David Minars
Professor of Economics
Brooklyn College

Accounting

Second Edition

All inquiries should be addressed to:
Barron's Educational Series, Inc.
250 Wireless Boulevard
Hauppauge, New York 11788
http://www.barronseduc.com

Library of Congress Catalog Card No. 2002034293

International Standard Book No. 0-7641-2001-8

Library of Congress Cataloging-in-Publication Data
Minars, David.
    Accounting / David Minars.—2nd ed.
        p. cm. — (Barron's EZ-101 study keys)
    Includes index.
    ISBN 0-7641-2001-8
    1   ys.
HF5(
657–   2002034293

PRIN
9 8 7 6 5

Preface

*B*arron's *EZ-101 Keys in Accounting* was written for both accounting and nonaccounting business students. The successful first edition of this text was written by Professor David Minars, an award-winning lecturer who has more than thirty years' experience teaching all phases of accounting, law, and federal taxation. This updated second edition can be used in conjunction with all current basic accounting texts. Its goal is to focus on the techniques that will enable a student to understand and record business transactions so that the resultant financial information can be used by management. A student using this text in an introductory accounting course will benefit because

1. accounting definitions are presented in clear and understandable terms;
2. the book provides a guide for learning and retaining basic accounting concepts and principles;
3. step-by-step "snapshot" examples of all required journal entries and supporting calculations are presented;
4. relevant examples are illustrated with straightforward clarity;
5. updated and current concepts reflecting the realities of today's global economy are discussed; and
6. this text uses short, direct sentences, which are more easily understood.

By using this book, all of a student's questions will be answered quickly and concisely. The amount of "pencil-pushing" time required to absorb conceptual material will be decreased. The final result of this unique approach will be a superb grasp of a student's assigned work, which is essential to success in any basic accounting course. Finally, the student's ability to pass his or her basic accounting course with a respectable grade will be greatly enhanced.

October 1, 2002

CONTENTS

Theme 1 ACCOUNTING AS AN INFORMATION SYSTEM

*A*ccounting is an information system that accumulates, records, classifies, summarizes, and reports commercial transactions with the aim of showing the financial condition of the business entity. This information, in the form of financial statements, is then communicated to those who make decisions concerning the operations of enterprise. Bookkeeping is a small part of this system and deals with repetitive record-keeping transactions.

INDIVIDUAL KEYS IN THIS THEME

1	Users of accounting information
2	Branches of accounting
3	Three basic forms of business organization
4	Accounting principles

Key 1   Users of accounting information

OVERVIEW *Accounting information is used by individuals and groups who must make decisions concerning the operations of an enterprise.*

Management: In order to maintain a profitable enterprise, management must maintain sufficient funds (called assets) to meet the entity's liabilities as they become due.

Investors: Virtually all businesses publish financial statements, which show the financial condition of the company and also indicate whether or not the company is making a profit.
- Investors use these statements to ascertain the strengths and weaknesses of the company.
- Potential creditors study these statements to determine whether the company has sufficient liquid assets, such as cash, with which to repay loans and other types of liabilities.

Society: Several groups in society, including the Internal Revenue Service, labor unions, and financial analysts, and the stock exchanges are interested in the profitability and operations of the entity.

Key 2   Branches of accounting

OVERVIEW *The major branches of accounting are public, private, and governmental accounting.*

Public accounting: The public accounting profession has achieved the same stature as medicine and law. Public accounting refers to the work done by independent Certified Public Accounting (CPA) firms that audit the books of companies to insure that their financial statements and records are not materially misstated.
- In order to become a licensed certified public accountant, an individual must pass the Uniform CPA Examination.
- CPAs are called upon to perform numerous services, including auditing, tax preparation, consulting, and advisory services.

Private accounting: Private accounting refers primarily to the private sector of the economy and involves the analysis and recording of financial information by accountants who are employees of the business entity.
- Private accountants work under the direct control of the chief accounting officer, who is called the controller.
- Private accountants, among their many duties, prepare budgets and departmental performance reports, which management uses to make managerial decisions.

Governmental accounting: This branch refers primarily to the accounting functions performed for federal, state, and local governmental institutions. Governmental accounting also includes the financial reporting functions applicable to hospitals, charitable organizations, colleges, and voluntary health and welfare organizations.

Key 3   Three basic forms of business
organization

OVERVIEW *The three basic forms of business organization are sole proprietorships, partnerships, and corporations.*

Sole proprietorship: A sole proprietorship is owned by one individual. The owner receives all profits, absorbs all losses, and is personally liable for any debts incurred by the business.

Partnership: A partnership is a business owned and operated by two or more individuals, called partners, who divide profits and losses according to some predetermined ratio. Each partner is personally liable for any debts incurred by the partnership.

Corporation: A corporation is owned by its stockholders, who purchase stock and elect a board of directors to manage the financial affairs of the business. Each stockholder enjoys limited liability and is personally liable only to the extent of his or her stock investment. These shares may be freely sold without affecting corporate operations.

The Limited Liability Company: A limited liability company (or "LLC") is a hybrid business organization that combines the characteristics of both corporations and partnerships.
The basic characteristics of the LLC are as follows:
- The owners are called "members" and not stockholders.
- The members enjoy the same limited liability as that of stockholders in a corporation.
- An LLC can be managed by all of its members, as in a partnership, or management can be centralized in one or more managers, as in a corporation.

Key 4   Accounting principles

OVERVIEW *Generally accepted accounting principles constitute acceptable accounting practice at a given time.*

Generally Accepted Accounting Principles (GAAP): Accounting theory provides a reasoning behind a framework for accounting practice. Generally accepted accounting principles are a set of guidelines and procedures that constitute acceptable accounting practice at a given time. They are developed by accountants and businesses to serve the needs of the users of the financial statements.
- Financial accounting requirements are announced by the Financial Accounting Standards Board (FASB), which is the principal rule-making body of the accounting profession.
- The pronouncements of the FASB are issued as FASB Statements and Interpretations.
- The American Institute of Certified Public Accountants (AICPA) issues Statements on Auditing Standards, which are guidelines that must be followed by independent CPAs who audit the financial records of their clients.
- The Securities and Exchange Commission (SEC) is an agency of the federal government that issues Accounting Series Releases, which dictate accounting practices for companies that sell stock to the public (called "public companies").

In response to the recent deluge of accounting and bankruptcy scandals affecting public companies, Congress passed the Sarbanes–Oxley Act of 2002. This act establishes new corporate governance standards, requires increased financial disclosure requirements, and now makes certain questionable accounting practices federal crimes.
- The Public Company Accounting Oversight Board (PCAOB) was created by the Sarbanes–Oxley Act to regulate and oversee audits of public companies by registered accounting firms.

Definitions: In order to generate information that is useful to the users of financial statements, accountants rely upon the following principles, assumptions, and definitions:
- *Comparability* means that the information is presented in such a way that the decision maker can recognize similarities, differences, and trends between different companies or between different time periods.
- *Consistency* requires that a particular accounting procedure, once adopted by a company, remain in use from one accounting period

to the next unless the users of the financial statements are informed of a change by means of notes to the financial statements.

- *Disclosure* requires that all relevant information that would influence the assessment of a company's health by outside users must be disclosed in the financial statements.
- *Materiality* refers to the relative importance of an item or event. If an item or event is material, it is likely to be relevant to the user of the financial statements.
- *Conservatism* means that when accountants face major uncertainties as to which accounting procedure to use, they generally choose a method that will understate assets and income.
- *Timeliness* requires that information generated by the accounting system must be received shortly after the end of the entity's accounting period in order to be useful for decision making.
- *Continuity,* also known as the going concern concept, assumes that the business will continue to operate indefinitely.
- *Entity* refers to the accounting unit or business, which is separate and apart from its owner or owners.
- *Accounting period* refers to the time span over which the accounting data is recorded and reported in the financial statements. Comparison of financial statements is made possible through the use of accounting periods of equal length. The time period could be one month, interim (three month), or annual (twelve month) financial statements. For most companies, the annual accounting period runs the calendar year from January 1 through December 31. Other companies use what is called a fiscal year, which ends on some date other than December 31.
- *Stable dollar theory* assumes that prices will remain constant over time. This theory requires that all assets be recorded at their historical cost.

Theme 2   PRINCIPLES OF ACCOUNTING AND FINANCIAL STATEMENTS

*U*nder the double entry system, each transaction must be recorded with a debit and a credit. Debit and credit postings are then made to a ledger account. At the end of an accounting period, balances are taken from each ledger account and are used to prepare financial statements. The four basic financial statements are the income statement, balance sheet, capital statement (statement of owner's equity), and the statement of cash flows.

Key 5   Accounting equation

OVERVIEW *The accounting equation states that assets must always equal creditors' claims and capital (owners' equity).*

Balance sheet: Presents two ways of viewing the same business.
- The left side shows the assets, resources owed by the business.
- The right side shows the obligations or liabilities owed by the company and its capital or owner's equity.
- The total dollar amount of assets must always be equal to the total dollar amount of the liabilities and capital.

This accounting equation is formally stated as

$$\text{Assets} = \text{Liabilities} + \text{Capital}$$
$$\text{or}$$
$$\text{Assets} - \text{Liabilities} = \text{Capital}$$

KEY EXAMPLE

If a business has assets of $100,000, liabilities of $60,000, and owner's equity of $40,000, the accounting equation is

$$\text{Assets} = \text{Liabilities} + \text{Capital}$$
$$\$100{,}000 = \$60{,}000 + \$40{,}000$$

Assets: The economic resources of the business.
- Assets that can be converted into cash within one year are classified as current assets. Examples: cash, accounts receivable, and inventory.
- Assets having a life that exceeds one year are classified as noncurrent. Examples: land, buildings, and patents.

Liabilities: The debts of the business.
- Those payable within one year are classified as current liabilities. *Examples:* money borrowed from banks, notes payable (maturity of one year or less), amounts owed to suppliers for goods bought on credit, salaries owed to workers, and taxes payable.
- Those payable over a period of more than one year are classified as noncurrent. Examples: bonds payable and long-term notes payable.

Capital (owner's equity): The owner's interest in the business; the difference between the assets and liabilities.

- In a sole proprietorship, there is only one capital account because there is only one owner.
- In a partnership, a capital account exists for each owner.
- Sole proprietors and partners are entitled to withdrawals from the business.
- In a corporation, capital or stockholders' equity consists of two accounts, capital stock outstanding plus the accumulated earnings of the business (called retained earnings).
- There are two types of capital stock—preferred stock and common stock. Preferred stock generally does not entitle its owner to voting rights; common stock does. Both are entitled to dividends.

Key 6   Double entry accounting

OVERVIEW *The accounting equation is the basis for double entry accounting, which means that every transaction has an effect on two or more accounts.*

KEY EXAMPLE

This example shows how transactions affect the accounting equation. Iris Nordquist finished medical school and immediately set up her own medical practice. During July, her first month of practice, she completed the following transactions:

Transaction 1: Began the practice of medicine by placing $10,000 in a bank account established for the medical practice.

Assets (A)	=	Liabilities (L)	+	Capital (C)
Cash				Capital
$10,000				$10,000

Transaction 2: Purchased equipment for $6,000.

	Assets (A)	=	Liabilities (L)	+	Capital (C)
	Cash + Equipment	=			Capital
	$10,000				$10,000
	(6,000) $6,000				
Balance	$4,000 $6,000				$10,000

Transaction 3: Purchased office supplies for $100 on credit.

		Assets (A) =	Liabilities (L)	+ Capital (C)
	Cash + Supp. +	Equipment =	Liabilities	+ Capital
Balance	$4,000	$6,000		$10,000
	$100		$100	
Balance	$4,000 $100	$6,000	$100	$10,000

Transaction 4: Received medical fees of $1,000.

		Assets (A) =	**Liabilities (L)**	**+ Capital (C)**
	Cash + Supp. +	Equipment =	Liabilities	+ Capital
Balance	$4,000 $100	$6,000	$100	$10,000
	1,000 100			1,000
Balance	$5,000 $100	$6,000	$100	$11,000

Transaction 5: Billed patients $1,500 for medical services performed during the month.

Assets (A) = Liabilities (L) + Capital (C)

	Cash +	A/R +	Supp. +	Equipment	=	Liabilities +	I. Nordquist Capital
Balance	$5,000		$100	$6,000		$100	$11,000
		$1,500					1,500
Balance	$5,000	$1,500	$100	$6,000		$100	$12,500

Transaction 6: Made partial payment of $50 for office supplies.

Assets (A) = Liabilities (L) + Capital (C)

	Cash +	A/R +	Supp. +	Equipment	=	Liabilities +	I. Nordquist Capital
Balance	$5,000	$1,500	$100	$6,000		$100	$12,500
	(50)					(50)	
Balance	$4,950	$1,500	$100	$6,000		$50	$12,500

Transaction 7: Paid rent expense of $1,000 for month.

Assets (A) = Liabilities (L) + Capital (C)

	Cash +	A/R +	Supp. +	Equipment	=	Liabilities +	I. Nordquist Capital
Balance	$4,950	$1,500	$100	$6,000		$50	$12,500
	(1,000)						(1,000)
Balance	$3,950	$1,500	$100	$6,000		$50	$11,500

Transaction 8: Withdrew $500 from practice for personal use.

Assets (A) = Liabilities (L) + Capital (C)

	Cash +	A/R +	Supp. +	Equipment	=	Liabilities +	I. Nordquist Capital
Balance	$3,950	$1,500	$100	$6,000		$50	$11,500
	(500)						(500)
Balance	$3,450	$1,500	$100	$6,000		$50	$11,000

Transaction 9: Paid monthly electric bill of $400.

Assets (A) = Liabilities (L) + Capital (C)

	Cash +	A/R +	Supp. +	Equipment	=	Liabilities +	I. Nordquist Capital
Balance	$3,450	$1,500	$100	$6,000		$50	$11,000
	(400)						(400)
Balance	$3,050	$1,500	$100	$6,000		$50	$10,600

Transaction 10: Paid monthly telephone bill of $100.

Assets (A) = Liabilities (L) + Capital (C)

	Cash +	A/R +	Supp. +	Equipment	=	Liabilities +	I. Nordquist Capital
Balance	$3,050	$1,500	$100	$6,000		$50	$10,600
	(100)						(100)
Balance	$2,950	$1,500	$100	$6,000		$50	$10,500

After recording all of the transactions, the accounting equation is still in balance. Assets totaling $10,550 ($2,950 + $1,500 + $100 + $6,000) still equal total liabilities and capital of $10,550 ($50 + $10,500).

A summary of the transactions would appear as follows:

Assets (A) = Liabilities (L) + Capital (C)

	Cash +	A/R +	Supp. +	Equipment	=	Liabilities +	I. Nordquist Capital	
1.	$10,000						$10,000	
2.	(6,000)			$6,000				
	$4,000			$6,000			$10,000	
3.			$100			$100		Supp.
	$4,000		$100	$6,000		$100	$10,000	
4.	1,000						1,000	Inc.
	$5,000		$100	$6,000		$100	$11,000	
5.		$1,500					1,500	Inc.
	$5,000	$1,500	$100	$6,000		$100	$12,500	
6.	(50)					(50)		
	$4,950	$1,500	$100	$6,000		$50	$12,500	
7.	(1,000)						(1,000)	Rent
	$3,950	$1,500	$100	$6,000		$50	$11,500	
8.	(500)						(500)	Draw
	$3,450	$1,500	$100	$6,000		$50	$11,000	
9.	(400)						(400)	Elec.
	$3,050	$1,500	$100	$6,000		$50	$10,600	
10.	(100)						(100)	Tel.
	$2,950	$1,500	$100	$6,000		$50	$10,500	

Key 7   Income statement

OVERVIEW *Accountants communicate their information through four basic financial statements: the income statement, balance sheet, capital statement (statement of owner's equity), and the statement of cash flows (see Theme 16).*

Income statement: The income statement is composed of revenues, expenses, and net income for a given period of time.

Revenues: Arise from either the sale of goods (inventory) or the performance of services, and usually results in an increase in either cash or accounts receivable.

Expenses: The cost of inventories sold, operating expenses such as rent, power, and maintenance, and salaries paid to workers during a specified period of time.

Net income: The amount by which total revenue exceeds total expenses for the reporting period.
- If revenues exceed expenses for the period, then capital will increase for the period.
- If expenses exceed revenues, thereby resulting in a net loss, capital will be decreased.

KEY EXAMPLE

Iris Nordquist, M.D.
Income Statement
for the Month Ended July 31, 2003

Revenue from Professional Services		$2,500
Less: Operating Expenses		
Rent Expense	$1,000	
Electric Expense	400	
Telephone Expense	100	1,500
Net Income		$1,000

Comprehensive income: Some accountants argue that rather than use a regular income statement whereby all revenues less expenses are used to arrive at net income, they prefer to use a comprehensive income statement. This type of statement includes not only net income, but all changes in the value of assets such as stock held by the company as an asset that has increased in value but has not yet been sold. The accepted accounting rule is that a company cannot record a gain or loss on another company's stock until it is sold.

KEY EXAMPLE

The income statement of Mars Inc., for the year 2003, appears as follows:

Sales	$90,000
Less: Expenses	70,000
Less: Net Income	$20,000

Mars Inc. also owns another company's stock that cost $20,000 but is now worth $23,000 at year-end. Thus the stock has increased by $3,000, which is called an unrealized gain because the company has not yet sold it. A company using the comprehensive presentation might present the income statement as follows:

Income Statement

Sales	$90,000
Less: Expenses	70,000
Less: Net Income	$20,000

Comprehensive Income Statement

Net Income	$20,000
Other Comprehensive Income	
Unrealized Gain on Stock	3,000
Comprehensive Income	$23,000

Key 8   Balance sheet

OVERVIEW *The balance sheet presents the financial position of the entity by listing the assets, liabilities, and capital at the end of the reporting period. The balance sheet is useful to management because it shows the resources of the business and what it owes to its creditors.*

KEY EXAMPLE

Iris Nordquist, M.D.
Balance Sheet
July 31, 2003

ASSETS			
Cash			$2,950
Accounts Receivable			1,500
Office Supplies			100
Office Equipment			6,000
Total Assets			$10,550
LIABILITIES			
Accounts Payable			$50
CAPITAL			
Investment, July 1		$10,000	
Net Income for July	$1,000		
Less: Withdrawals	500		
Increase in Capital		500	
Total Capital			10,500
Total Liabilities and Capital			$10,550

Key 9   Capital statement

OVERVIEW *The capital statement, also known as the statement of owner's equity, ties the income statement to the balance sheet by showing how the owner's equity changes during the period.*

Recording changes in capital:
- The owner's capital at the beginning of the period is the first item on the statement.
- The net income for the accounting period is then added to the beginning capital, as are any additional investments made during the period.
- Finally, any withdrawals by the owner during the period are subtracted, as is a net loss, to arrive at the owner's capital at the end of the period.

Example: From the balance sheet presented in Key 8, it is evident that Nordquist's net income of $1,000 (from her income statement) has been added to her beginning capital investment of $10,000. Her withdrawals of $500 were then subtracted from net income to arrive at her final capital balance of $10,500.

Key 10 Corporate stockholders' equity

OVERVIEW *Corporate stockholders' equity consists of outstanding stock (contributed capital) and retained earnings.*

Stockholders' equity: If we are accounting for a corporation, the ownership section of the balance sheet would be designated as stockholders' equity (owner's equity or capital), and would consist of common stock issued and retained earnings.

KEY EXAMPLE

The Ramirez Corporation issued common stock for $10,000. Assume that the company also had retained earnings of $5,000 on November 1. If the corporation earned $13,400 for the month and paid $2,000 in dividends, the ending stockholders' equity section of the balance sheet would show the following:

Ramirez Corporation
Stockholders' Equity
for the Period Ended November 30

Common Stock	$10,000
Retained Earnings	16,400
Total Stockholders' Equity	$26,400

Payment of dividends: Dividends represent a distribution of profits after taxes. Dividends paid to stockholders come out of retained earnings. The payment of dividends is a reduction of owner's equity and not an expense.

KEY EXAMPLE

A statement of retained earnings for the period would show the following activities in that account:

Ramirez Corporation
Statement of Retained Earnings
for the Period Ended November 30

Retained Earnings November 1	$5,000
Net Income for the Period	13,400
Subtotal	$18,400
Less: Dividends	2,000
Retained Earnings, November 30	$16,400

Theme 3   RECORDING BUSINESS TRANSACTIONS

*A*n account is a device used to record financial data. Each asset, liability, and component of owner's equity, as well as income and expenses, has a separate ledger account. At the end of an accounting period, the debit or credit balance is determined in each ledger account and a trial balance is prepared to test whether the total of the debit balances equals the total of the credit balances in the ledger.

INDIVIDUAL KEYS IN THIS THEME
11   The account
12   General ledger
13   Posting entries from the journal to the accounts
14   Ledger accounts after posting
15   Preparing a trial balance

Key 11　The account

OVERVIEW　*The basic summary device of accounting is the account. It resembles the letter T, and its left side is called the debit side and its right side the credit side.*

Double entry system: A system of accounting requires that for each recorded transaction there must be one or more accounts debited and one or more accounts credited. The total debits for the transaction must always equal the total credits.

Meaning of debits and credits: In order to determine which accounts are to be debited or credited in a given transaction, the following rules should be followed:

Debits	Credits
a. Increase assets	a. Decrease assets
b. Decrease liabilities	b. Increase liabilities
c. Increase withdrawals	c. Increase capital
d. Increase expenses	d. Increase revenue

Key 12   General ledger

OVERVIEW *All of a company's accounts are contained in a book called a general ledger, or simply the ledger.*

The ledger: The ledger is the group of actual accounts.
- Balance sheet accounts are classified as assets, liabilities, and owner's equity.
- Income statement accounts are classified as revenues or expenses.
- Each account is customarily listed on a separate page in the general ledger in the order in which they appear in the financial statements.
- A listing of all the accounts, with their respective account numbers, is called a chart of accounts. Each account has a separate page in the manual general ledger.

Key 13 — Posting entries from the journal to the accounts

OVERVIEW *Accountants first record all transactions in a journal, often called "the book of original entry." Journal entries are posted from the journal to the appropriate ledger accounts.*

Journal: As transactions occur, they are initially recorded in a journal. The general journal is the simplest type of journal and can be used to record all types of transactions.

Specialized journals: These include a cash receipts journal, which records all cash received by a business, and a sales journal, which is used to record all sales. Specialized journals are used to record repetitive transactions.

Entries: Each journal entry (transaction) is journalized (recorded) in the journal and contains (1) date, (2) the account names, (3) the dollar amounts debited and credited, (4) an explanation, (5) the account numbers, and (6) an appropriate explanation.
- A journal entry containing two or more debits or two or more credits is called a compound entry.
- A line should be skipped after each journal entry.

Posting: The information in the journal entry is transferred from the journal to the ledger by debiting and crediting the particular accounts involved, a process called posting.

Headings: Headings found in the typical general journal would appear as follows:

General Journal

Date	Accounts and Explanations	Account Number	Debit	Credit
200X				

Making journal entries: This procedure is shown in the example below. The account number column represents the numbers assigned to each account under the chart of accounts numbering system. Note that dollar signs are not used when making or posting journal entries.

Kate Bexar, a lawyer, began her law practice on April 1.

1. On April 1, Bexar, a sole proprietor, invested $40,000 in her law practice. *Analysis:* An entry must be made in the general journal, which records a debit to cash, as asset, and a credit to Kate Bexar, capital, for $40,000. The entry amounts will then be posted from the journal to the appropriate ledger accounts.

Date	Accounts and Explanations	P.R.	Debit	Credit
April 1	Cash	1	40,000	
	Kate Bexar, Capital	26		40,000
	To record initial investment by owner.			

Cash 1		Kate Bexar, Capital 26	
(1) 40,000			(1) 40,000

2. On April 2, Bexar paid rent of $500. *Analysis:* An entry must be made in the general ledger debiting rent expense and crediting cash for $500.

Date	Accounts and Explanations	P.R.	Debit	Credit
April 2	Rent Expense	36	500	
	Cash	1		500
	To record payment for rent for April.			

Rent Expense 36		Cash 1	
(2) 500		(1) 40,000	(2) 500

Key 14   Ledger accounts after posting

OVERVIEW *At the end of an accounting period, one must determine account balances in order to prepare the financial statements.*

Determining the balance: At the end of an accounting period, the debit and credit balances in each account must be determined in order to prepare a trial balance.
- Each balance is determined by footing (adding up) all the debits and credits in each account.
- If the debits in the account are more than the credits, then the account is said to have a debit balance.
- If the credits exceed the debits, the account is said to have a credit balance.

KEY EXAMPLE

The account balances at April 30 for Kate Bexar will appear as follows:

Cash 1		Kate Bexar, Capital 26	
(1) 40,000	(2) 500		(1) 40,000
Balance 39,500			Balance 40,000

Rent Expense 36	
(2) 500	
Balance 500	

Key 15 Preparing a trial balance

OVERVIEW *Before preparing financial statements, the accountant must double-check the equality of the debits and credits in the accounts. This is done by preparing a trial balance.*

Trial balance: This is a list of all accounts with their balances.

Errors: If the debits and credits are not equal, an error has been made. *Example:* A debit may have been posted as a credit, or an account may have been improperly footed.
- A trial balance would not disclose whether an entry were incorrectly entered in an expense account rather than in an asset account.
- A trial balance would not show that an entry had been omitted from the ledger.

KEY EXAMPLE

Kate Bexar, Attorney at Law
Trial Balance
April 30

Account Titles	Debit	Credit
Cash...	$37,600	$
Office Equipment.............................	2,400	
Office Supplies..................................	300	
Accounts Payable..............................		200
Kate Bexar, Capital...........................		40,000
Withdrawals	1,000	
Professional Fee Income....................		1,700
Rent Expense	500	
Cleaning and Maintenance.................	100	
Total..	$41,900	$41,900

Once all errors have been located and the trial balance is in balance, the financial statements can be prepared.

Theme 4   COMPLETION OF THE ACCOUNTING CYCLE— ADJUSTING AND CLOSING ENTRIES

*U*nder the matching principle, revenues must be assigned to the period in which they are earned and expenses must be assigned to the accounting period in which they were used to produce revenue. In order to apply the matching rule, adjusting entries are required at the end of an accounting period. These entries are used to apportion income and expenses between two or more accounting periods, to record expenses incurred but not paid for the period, and to record revenues earned but not yet received. After the accounts have been adjusted, closing entries transfer revenue, expense, and owner withdrawal balances from their respective accounts to the owner's capital account.

INDIVIDUAL KEYS IN THIS THEME

16 Revenues and expenses

17 Prepaid expenses

18 Unearned revenues

19 Accrued expenses

20 Accrued revenues

21 Adjusting for depreciation

22 Closing entries

23 Post-closing trial balance

Key 16   Revenues and expenses

OVERVIEW *The goal of all businesses is to earn a profit. Net income results when revenues exceed expenses, and a net loss occurs when expenses exceed revenues.*

Revenue: Revenue is normally earned when goods or services are provided.

Expenses: Expenses are recognized when incurred regardless of when they are paid in cash. A problem arises when revenues or expenses apply to more than one period. This problem is solved by making adjusting entries at the end of the reporting period to record the correct income and expenses for the period.

Adjusting entries: The four basic adjusting entries relate to prepaid or unexpired costs, unearned or deferred income revenue, accrued expenses incurred but not paid, and accrued revenue that is earned but will not be received until the following accounting period.

Key 17 Prepaid expenses

OVERVIEW *A prepaid expense account is debited when an expense is paid in advance.*

Prepaid expense: An expenditure made in the current period that will benefit both the current and future periods.
- The initial debit is made to an asset account.
- At the end of the accounting period, an adjusting entry is made that records, in an expense account, the amount that has been used up or has expired for the accounting period.

KEY EXAMPLE

On January 1, the Rex Company bought a two-year insurance policy for $2,000. The general journal entry at January 1 would appear as follows:

Jan. 1	Prepaid Insurance	2,000	
	Cash		2,000

At the end of the year, the following adjusting journal entry to record the amount of insurance that has expired and must be reclassified an expense would appear as follows:

Dec. 31	Insurance Expense	1,000	
	Prepaid Insurance		1,000
	To record one year's insurance that has expired.		

After posting, the prepaid insurance account, which is a current asset, would appear as follows:

Prepaid Insurance			
Jan. 1	2,000	Dec. 31	1,000
Balance	1,000		

Key 18   Unearned revenues

OVERVIEW *When payment is received in advance for goods before they are delivered or for services before they are rendered, an account called unearned revenue must be recorded.*

Unearned revenue: Unearned revenue is a current liability account that must appear at year-end on the balance sheet. The liability arises because the business receiving the payment is obligated to either deliver goods or perform services in the future.

KEY EXAMPLE

On December 1, the Rambeau Window Washing Company received $300 in advance for services to be performed for December, January, and February. The company's year-end is December 31. The general journal entry to record the $300 advance payment would be as follows:

Dec. 1	Cash	300	
	Unearned Revenue		300
	To record revenue for the period December		
	through February received in advance.		

At the end of the year, the following adjusting journal entry to record the amount of revenue that was earned for December would appear as follows:

Dec. 31	Unearned Revenue	100	
	Revenue From Services		100
	To record revenue earned for month		
	of December.		

After posting, the unearned revenue account, which is a current liability, would appear as follows:

Unearned Revenue			
Dec. 31	100	Dec. 1	300
		Balance	200

Key 19   Accrued expenses

OVERVIEW *An accrued expense is an expense incurred, but not paid, in the current period.*

Adjusting entry: An unrecorded expense that has been incurred in the current accounting period but will not be paid by the end of the accounting period requires an adjusting entry, which means a debit to an expense account and a credit to a current liability account.

KEY EXAMPLE

On December 1, 2003, the Enright Company borrowed $10,000. The company agreed to pay interest at the rate of 1% per month. The note is due on February 28, 2004. The adjusting entry at December 31, 2003, would be as follows:

Dec. 31, 2003	Interest Expense	100	
	Interest Payable		100
	To record accrued interest for one month		
	($10,000 × 1% = $100).		

Assume that Enright had, during the year, already paid $5,000 in interest expenses. After posting, the interest expense account would appear as follows:

	Interest Expense	
	5,000	
Dec. 31	100	

Key 20   Accrued revenues

OVERVIEW *Revenue that has been earned, but not yet received in cash, is called accrued revenue.*

Adjusting entry: Accrued or unrecorded revenue represents revenue that has been earned but not yet collected by the end of the accounting period. An adjusting entry must be made at the end of the accounting period to record the revenue earned but not yet received. The adjusting entry debits an asset account and credits an appropriate revenue account.

KEY EXAMPLE

At December 31, the Colby Real Estate Company had not received its rent of $1,000 from a tenant for the month of December. The adjusting journal entry at December 31, the end of the accounting period, would be as follows:

Dec. 31	Rent Receivable	1,000	
	Rental Income		1,000
	To record December rent.		

Assume that Colby had, during the year, already received $100,000 in rental income from other tenants. After posting, the rental income account would appear as follows:

Rental Income	
	100,000
	Dec. 31 1,000

Key 21   Adjusting for depreciation

OVERVIEW *Plant assets are long-lived assets, such as land and buildings, furniture, and machinery and equipment used in the operations of the business. All plant assets, except for land, are subject to depreciation.*

Accumulated depreciation: This is a contra-asset account.
- Year-end adjusting entries for depreciation are similar to those made for reducing a prepaid expense account whereby a debit is made to an expense account and the credit reduces the asset account.
- The principal difference is that the credit is made to an account called accumulated depreciation.
- Accumulated depreciation, a contra asset account, appears as a subtraction from the asset to which the depreciation is applicable.

KEY EXAMPLE

On January 1, the Jeremy Company bought a machine for $10,000. Depreciation for the year was $1,000. The adjusting journal entry to record depreciation on the machine at year-end would be as follows:

Dec. 31	Depreciation Expense	1,000	
	Accumulated Depreciation		1,000
	To record depreciation on machine for the year.		

Both accounts at year-end would appear as follows:

Depreciation Expense		Accumulated Depreciation	
Dec. 31 1,000			Dec. 31 1,000

At December 31, the machine would appear on the balance sheet as follows:

Machine	$10,000
Less: Accumulated Depreciation	1,000
Book Value	$ 9,000

Key 22   Closing entries

OVERVIEW   *Closing entries transfer revenue, expense, and owner withdrawal balances from their respective accounts to the owner's capital account.*

Closing entries: Apply only to nominal or temporary accounts:
- Both revenue and expense accounts are temporary or nominal accounts and must be closed out.
- The balances in these accounts must be transferred to an intermediate account called Income Summary.
- The balance in this account is then transferred either to owner's capital or, in the case of a corporation, to an account called retained earnings.

Owner's withdrawal account: Although not a revenue or expense account, an owner's withdrawal account is temporary because it records the amount of money withdrawn for the period by the owner.
- This account, which appears only in the accounts of either a sole proprietorship or a partnership, must be closed into owner's capital.

Permanent or real accounts: Assets, liabilities, and capital are permanent or real accounts and are never closed out at the end of the accounting period.

KEY EXAMPLE

The journal entry to close out rental income into the Income Summary account at year-end would be as follows:

Dec. 31	Rental Income	XXX	
	Income Summary		XXX
	To close Rental Income into Income Summary.		

The journal entry to close out expenses into the income summary at year-end would be as follows:

Dec. 31	Income Summary	XXX	
	Expenses		XXX
	To close Expenses into Income Summary.		

After closing, all revenue and expense accounts will have a zero balance. If after closing all income and expenses into Income Summary, the account had a credit balance, this would indicate a profit. The following entry would then be made:

Dec. 31	Income Summary	XXX	
	Capital		XXX
	To close Income Summary into Capital.		

If after closing all income and expenses into the Income Summary, the account had a debit balance, this would indicate a loss. The following entry would then be made:

Dec. 31	Capital	XXX	
	Income Summary		XXX
	To close Income Summary into Capital.		

The final closing entry would close the Withdrawals account into the capital account and would appear as follows:

Dec. 31	Capital	XXX	
	Withdrawals		XXX
	To close the Withdrawal account into Capital.		

Note that the Income Summary account is not involved in this closing entry.

Key 23   Post-closing trial balance

OVERVIEW *The accounting cycle begins with the analysis and journalizing of transactions and ends with the post-closing trial balance.*

Accounting cycle: The accounting cycle ends with the post-closing trial balance.
- The post-closing trial balance verifies that all the debits equal the credits in the trial balance.
- The trial balance contains only balance sheet items such as assets, liabilities, and ending capital because all income and expense accounts, as well as the withdrawal account, have zero balances.

KEY EXAMPLE

Jack Moxie Company
Trial Balance
December 31

Cash	$ 6,000	
Accounts Receivable	7,000	
Plant	100,000	
Machinery	17,000	
Accumulated Depreciation		$ 10,000
Land	20,000	
Accounts Payable		40,000
Jack Moxie, Capital		70,000
Jack Moxie, Withdrawals	4,000	
Service Revenue		60,000
Salaries Expense	7,000	
Electricity Expense	5,000	
Rent Expense	9,000	
Depreciation Expense	5,000	
	$180,000	$180,000

The closing entries in the general journal at December 31 would appear as follows:

Dec. 31   Service Revenue   60,000
              Income Summary   60,000
           To close Service Revenue into Income Summary.

Dec. 31	Income Summary	26,000	
	Salaries Expense		7,000
	Electricity Expense		5,000
	Rent Expense		9,000
	Depreciation Expense		5,000
	To close expenses into Income Summary.		

The Income Summary account would then appear as follows:

Income Summary

| Closing 26,000 | Closing 60,000 |
| Balance 34,000 | |

Dec. 31	Income Summary	34,000	
	Capital		34,000
	To close Income Summary into Capital.		

Dec. 31	Capital	4,000	
	Withdrawals		4,000
	To close the Withdrawal account into Capital.		

The post-closing trial balance, consisting of only real or permanent accounts, would appear as follows:

Jack Moxie Company
Post-Closing Trial Balance
December 31

Cash	$ 6,000	
Accounts Receivable	7,000	
Plant	100,000	
Machinery	17,000	
Accumulated Depreciation		$ 10,000
Land	20,000	
Accounts Payable		40,000
Jack Moxie, Capital		100,000
	$150,000	$150,000

Theme 5   HOW TO PREPARE A
WORKSHEET AND
FINANCIAL STATEMENTS

A worksheet is prepared at the end of an accounting period. It brings together, in one place, all of the transactions of a particular period so that the financial data can be used in the preparation of the financial statements.

Key 24   Worksheet

OVERVIEW *The worksheet is a tool used to help the accountant move the information from the trial balance to the completed financial statements. The worksheet is not part of any ledger, nor is it presented along with the financial statements.*

Worksheet as a summary device: The accountant generally prepares a worksheet at the end of an accounting period. The worksheet brings together, in one place, all of the transactions of a particular period so that the financial data can be used in the preparation of the financial statements.

- It provides an efficient way for the accountant to (1) make all required adjusting journal entries, and (2) identify and classify all accounts that make up both the income statement and balance sheet.
- The worksheet also helps the accountant to discover existing posting and calculation errors.

Key 25 Preparing a worksheet for a service business

OVERVIEW *The unadjusted or opening trial balance is prepared in the first two columns of the worksheet. Adjustments are then made to the accounts to arrive at an adjusted trial balance. Account balances from the adjusted trial balance then go either to the income statement or to balance sheet columns.*

Preparing a worksheet: The preparation of the worksheet provides a quick review of all of the ledger balances as well as the adjusting journal entries.
- The trial balance is prepared in pencil directly on the worksheet.
- The adjusting entries are then prepared in the Adjustments column.
- The accountant will then check to see whether the debits equal the credits. If the debits do not equal the credits, the error must first be found before any further work can be done on the worksheet.
- The accounts found in the Adjusted Trial Balance column will then go to either the income statement or the balance sheet columns, but not to both.
- The heading on the top of the worksheet names the business, identifies the document, and states the accounting period.
- The columns of a typical worksheet appear in the following order: trial balance, adjustments, adjusted trial balance, income statement, and balance sheet.

KEY EXAMPLE

Account Title	Trial Balance	Adjustments	Adjusted Trial Balance	Income Statement	Balance Sheet
	Dr. Cr.	Dr. Cr.	Dr. Cr.	Dr. Cr.	Dr. Cr.

Key 26   Using the worksheet to prepare the financial statements

OVERVIEW *Transfer the account balances from the adjusted trial balance on the worksheet to the Income Statement and Balance Sheet columns. Then total the Income Statement columns to determine whether the company has net income or a net loss for the period. As the final step, transfer the income or loss figure to the balance sheet columns and recompute the column totals.*

KEY EXAMPLE

Cedric Barnes owned and operated the Cedric Office Cleaning Company. The unadjusted trial balance of the company at September 30, the end of the company's fiscal year, appears as follows:

Cash	$ 7,000	
Accounts Receivable	10,000	
Cleaning Supplies	600	
Prepaid Insurance	1,000	
Plant	100,000	
Machinery	20,000	
Accumulated Depreciation		$ 32,000
Accounts Payable		9,000
Unearned Service Income		13,600
Cedric Barnes, Capital		50,000
Cedric Barnes, Withdrawals	25,000	
Income From Cleaning Services		100,000
Salary Expense	28,000	
Rent Expense	8,000	
Insurance Expense	1,000	
Telephone Expense	2,600	
Miscellaneous Expenses	1,400	
	$204,600	$204,600

Adjustments: The accountant determined that the following year-end adjustments were also required:
- Accrued salaries payable amounted to $1,000.
- Prepaid insurance expired during the period was $500.
- Cleaning supplies used for the period amounted to $200.
- $10,000 of the unearned service revenue was earned for the fiscal year.
- Annual depreciation on plant and machinery was $6,000.

Based on the above information, the accountant would take the following steps in order to prepare the company's fiscal year financial statements:

Step 1: Enter the trial balance amounts, in pencil, on the worksheet.

Step 2: Make the required year-end adjusting entries on the worksheet. The sequence of the adjustments is not important. Cross-referencing the related debit and credit of each adjusting journal entry is useful to anyone who might have to review the worksheet. Based on the above information, the following adjusting entries would be required:

- Accrued salaries payable amounted to $1,000.

Sept. 30	Salary Expense	1,000	
	Accrued Salaries Payable		1,000

- Prepaid insurance expired was $500.

Sept. 30	Insurance Expense	500	
	Prepaid Insurance		500

- Cleaning supplies used for the period amounted to $200.

Sept. 30	Cleaning Supplies Expense	200	
	Cleaning Supplies		200

- $10,000 of the unearned service revenue was earned for the fiscal year.

Sept. 30	Unearned Service Income	10,000	
	Service Income		10,000

- Annual depreciation on plant and machinery was $6,000

Sept. 30	Depreciation Expense	6,000	
	Accumulated Depreciation		6,000

Step 3: After the adjusting entries have been reflected on the worksheet, and all columns have been checked to see that they balance, the account balances are extended from the adjusted trial balance columns to the income statements and balance sheet columns.

- After totaling the Income Statement and Balance Sheet columns, enter the net income or net loss in both pairs of columns as a balancing figure.
- If the total of the credits in the income statement column is more than the total of the debits, the business has earned a profit.
- If the total of the debits in the income statement column is more than the total of the credits, the business has a loss for the period.
- The fact that the totals in each pair of columns equal each other is not an absolute proof of accuracy. Note that Withdrawals are shown in the debit column of the balance sheet since withdrawals are not expenses, but personal distributions of assets to the owner. If an asset has been carried to the debit column of the income statement, the worksheet will still balance, but the income statement will be wrong.

Step 4: After completion of the worksheet, prepare the financial statements. This is a simple procedure because the account balances have been sorted into Income Statement and Balance Sheet columns.

Cedric Office Cleaning Company
Trial Balance
September 30, 2003

Account Title	Trial Balance Dr.	Trial Balance Cr.	Adjustments Dr.	Adjustments Cr.	Adjusted Trial Balance Dr.	Adjusted Trial Balance Cr.	Income Statement Dr.	Income Statement Cr.	Balance Sheet Dr.	Balance Sheet Cr.
Cash	7,000				7,000				7,000	
Accounts Receivable	10,000				10,000				10,000	
Cleaning Supplies	600			(c)200	400				400	
Prepaid Insurance	1,000			(f)500	500				500	
Plant	100,000				100,000				100,000	
Machinery	20,000				20,000				20,000	
Accumulated Depreciation		32,000		(e)6,000		38,000				38,000
Accounts Payable		9,000				9,000				9,000
Unearned Service Income		13,600	(d)10,000			3,600				3,600
Cedric Barnes, Capital		50,000				50,000				50,000
Cedric Barnes, Withdrawals	25,000				25,000				25,000	
Income		100,000		(d)10,000		110,000		110,000		
Salary Expense	28,000		(a)1,000		29,000		29,000			
Rent Expense	8,000				8,000		8,000			
Insurance Expense	1,000		(f)500		1,500		1,500			
Telephone Expense	2,600				2,600		2,600			
Miscellaneous Expense	1,400				1,400		1,400			
	204,600	204,600								
Accrued Salaries Payable				(a)1,000		1,000				1,000
Cleaning Supplies Expense			(c)200		200		200			
Depreciation Expense			(e)6,000		6,000		6,000			
			17,700	17,700	211,600	211,600	48,700	110,000	162,900	101,600
NET INCOME							61,300			61,300
							110,000	110,000	162,900	162,900

42

Key 27   Classification of assets and liabilities on the balance sheet

OVERVIEW *On the balance sheet, assets and liabilities are classified as either current or long term to indicate their relative liquidity. Liquidity is a measure of how quickly an item can be converted into cash.*

Current assets: These assets can be expected to be converted into cash within the next twelve months or within the business's normal operating cycle if longer than a year. *Cash, accounts receivable, notes receivable* due within one year, and prepaid expenses are current assets. If a business is involved in merchandising (the sale of goods), the balance sheet contains an additional current asset, *inventory.*

Long-term assets: These assets include *land, buildings, furniture and fixtures, machinery,* and *notes receivable* due after one year.

Current liabilities: These are debts that are due to be paid within one year or within the business's normal operating cycle if longer. *Notes payable, accounts payable, taxes payable,* and *salaries payable* are examples of current liabilities.

Long-term liabilities: These liabilities are not classified as current. They consist of long-term *notes payable* and *mortgage notes payable.*

Key 28   Preparation of the financial statements from the worksheet

OVERVIEW *The worksheet provides the information needed for preparation of the financial statements without reference to the ledger or other records.*

Preparation of the financial statements: The financial statements prepared from the worksheet include a Statement of Income, a Statement of Capital, and a Balance Sheet.

KEY EXAMPLE

Cedric Office Cleaning Company
Income Statement
For Year Ending September 30, 2003

Cleaning Service Income		$110,000
Less: Expenses		
Salary Expense	$29,000	
Rent Expense	8,000	
Telephone Expense	2,600	
Insurance Expense	1,500	
Cleaning Supplies Expense	200	
Depreciation Expense	6,000	
Miscellaneous Expense	1,400	
Total Expenses		48,700
Net income		$ 61,300

Statement of Owner's Equity

Cedric Barnes, Capital, October 1, 2002	$ 50,000
Net Income	61,300
Subtotal	$111,300
Less: Withdrawals	25,000
Cedric Barnes, Capital, September 30, 2003	$ 86,300

Balance Sheet

ASSETS

Current Assets

Cash	$ 7,000	
Accounts Receivable	10,000	
Cleaning Supplies	400	
Prepaid Insurance	500	
Total Current Assets		$17,900

Long-Term Assets

Plant	$100,000	
Machinery	20,000	
	$120,000	
Less: Accumulated Depreciation	38,000	82,000
Total Assets		$99,900

LIABILITIES AND CAPITAL

Current Liabilities

Accounts Payable	$9,000	
Accrued Salaries Payable	1,000	
Unearned Income	3,600	
Total Current Liabilities		$13,600

Capital

Cedric Barnes, Capital		86,300
Total Liabilities and Capital		$99,900

Theme 6   COMPUTERIZED
ACCOUNTING SYSTEMS

*V*irtually all businesses use a computerized accounting system. The computer system is the information center used to internally record all financial information. The system may also have links with other companies who may do business with the company such as customers and sellers of goods and services. The use of computers will continue to grow as companies expand globally, using their Internet capabilities. Most small companies use a PC or microcomputer for their basic computer needs. A computer and a modem are needed to connect to the Internet, the world's largest computer network.

INDIVIDUAL KEYS IN THIS THEME

Key 29   Components of a computer system

OVERVIEW *A computer system is composed of various integrated units. Each unit is dependent upon the other segments for support. A basic system will include hardware, software, and support personnel. Virtually all computers used in business are connected to the Internet, the world's largest computer network.*

Hardware: Hardware consists of the physical equipment needed to operate a computer system. Input data is done through the keyboard, which is communicated to the central processing unit (CPU) or network server for processing and storing data. Use of a PC permits accountants to input financial information into general ledger and spreadsheet software. At the end of an accounting period such as a month, quarter, or year-end, printed financial reports can be generated from the general ledger or spreadsheet program for use by management.

Software: A program that contains a set of instructions and steps that allow a computer to configure data into a desired format such as a balance sheet, income statement, or statement of cash flows is called software. Other software programs generate various charts and statements used by management such as sales charts indicating growth and cash budgets. Typical software programs used by accountants are Peachtree Complete Accounting for Windows and QuickBooks.

Personnel: Key personnel needed to run a computer system are the systems analyst, programmer, and computer operator. The systems analyst designs the program, the programmer writes the instruction for a required program, and the computer operator inputs the required data. Companies often consult with outside experts such as Certified Public Accountants (CPAs) when setting up the basic accounting system.

The Internet: A computer system allows individuals, including accountants and businesses, access to a vast amount of information. Businesses use the **Internet** to establish web sites advertising their goods and services. The Internet also allows the sending of electronic mail (e-mail) to individuals and businesses. To use the Internet, a computer must have a modem and a number for the modem to call. An Internet service provider (ISP) such as America Online (AOL) connects the computer to the Internet.

Key 30   Spreadsheets

OVERVIEW *A spreadsheet is required for any accounting system using a double entry accounting method. The spreadsheet saves time over manual preparation by allowing the input of critical data that is automatically analyzed and reconfigured into useful data.*

Spreadsheet programs: A spreadsheet consists of a grid made up of columns into which numbers and other financial data are entered to create financial documents. Spreadsheet programs have a definite advantage over the manual preparation of a worksheet in that any changes can be inserted immediately and spreadsheet results are then updated automatically. This means that when extensions to the other columns are made, all column totals and net income is recomputed instantly. Of course, the software is purely a mechanical tool and trained personnel are necessary for inserting the information correctly. Microsoft Excel and Lotus are popular spreadsheet programs used by accountants and other financial planners. In virtually all accounting computer programs, a debit carries a positive sign, whereas a credit is always posted as a negative.

Theme 7   PROCESSING CASH
RECEIPTS

*M*ost business transactions are carried out by cash, the most liquid of all assets. Cash is generally classified as a current asset and must be readily available for the payment of current liabilities such as accounts, notes, taxes, and salaries payable.

INDIVIDUAL KEYS IN THIS THEME

OVERVIEW *Most business transactions are carried out by cash, although businesses commonly maintain small petty cash funds for making small payments. Companies frequently have excess cash that they invest in short-term or marketable securities. A company's assets, including its cash, are protected by internal controls.*

Internal controls: Detailed procedures are adopted by an enterprise to ensure accurate accounting records, safeguard a company's assets, and promote operational efficiency. Internal control requires a separation of employee duties so that employee opportunities for committing fraud are minimized.

Cash: Cash consists of coins and currency on hand, checks, money orders, savings deposits, and bank deposits. Postage stamps, postdated checks (checks bearing a future date at which time the check is to be deposited), and IOUs are not treated as cash. To protect cash, all businesses set up a bank account.

Bank account: A major method for maintaining control over cash is the bank account. The documents used to control a bank account include the signature card, the deposit ticket, the check, the bank statement, and the bank reconciliation.
- To get the most benefit from a bank account, all cash received must be deposited in the bank account and all payments must be made by checks drawn on the account.
- Keeping cash in a bank account is part of internal control because banks have established practices for safeguarding cash.
- A bank account permits a double record of cash, one maintained by the business and the other by the bank.

Key 32 Bank reconciliation

OVERVIEW *There are two records of a company's cash: its cash account in the general ledger and the bank statement. The two balances are rarely in agreement.*

The bank statement: This monthly statement mailed by the bank to the business indicates what the business has in its cash account.

The general ledger: This records the day-to-day transactions of the business.

Reasons for discrepancies:
- Deposits in transit. The business has made a deposit at the end of the month that will be recorded by the bank in the following month.
- Outstanding checks. Checks have been drawn by the business and mailed but have not yet been paid by the bank and are treated as outstanding checks. A certified check is never outstanding. When a bank has agreed to certify a check, it immediately charges the depositor's account for the amount of the check prior to its mailing.
- Bank charges. These are charges recorded by the bank and charged against the customer's account for bank services, printing checks, and non-sufficient funds (NSF) checks. The customer is usually not aware of these charges until after it receives the monthly bank statement.
- Collection of a note. The bank may have collected a note for the depositor that has not been recorded in the ledger.
- Errors. May include the depositor's incorrectly recording the amount of a check, or the bank's charging the customer's account for a check drawn by another depositor.

Key 33   Preparation of bank
reconciliation

OVERVIEW *The form of the bank reconciliation consists of two sections: (1) Balance per bank statement and (2) Balance per depositor's books.*

KEY EXAMPLE

The bank statement of the Hello Company indicated a balance of $4,360 as of December 31. The balance in the Cash account in Hello's general ledger on the same date showed an uncorrected balance of $3,397. A further investigation indicated the following reconciling items and errors:
- Hello's $900 deposit of December 31 was not recorded until January 3 of the following year.
- The following checks were outstanding at December 31:

Check No.		
7004	$1,500	
7006	300	
7014	122	

- The bank collected a note of $240. The note included interest of $20.
- Bank service charges for the month of December were $10. These charges had not been recorded on Hello's books as of December 31.
- Hello's bookkeeper recorded, on the books of the company, check number 7007 as $66. The correct amount was $55.
- The bank erroneously charged Hello's bank account for a $100 check drawn by Hett Company, another depositor.
- A check for $200 received from the Otto Company was returned marked "Unpaid Due To Insufficient Funds."

The bank reconciliation, based on the bank statement and the reconciling items, would appear as follows

Balance per bank statement at the end of period		$4,360
Add: Deposit in transit:	$900	

Bank error—incorrect check belonging to Hett Company charged to account	100	1,000
		$5,360
Deduct: Outstanding checks		
Check No. 7004	$1,500	
7006	300	
7014	122	1,922
Correct cash balance		$3,438
Balance per books (uncorrected)		$3,397
Add: Note collected by bank	$220	
Interest on note collected by bank	20	
Error in recording check No. 7007	11	251
		$3,648
Deduct: Bank service charges	10	
NSF check returned	200	210
Correct cash balance		$3,438

Journal entries: Certain journal entries may be required upon completion of the bank reconciliation. Entries are usually recorded for bank service charges, the collection of notes by the bank on behalf of the depositor, and charges for unpaid checks received from customers.

Example:

Cash	240	
Notes Receivable		220
Interest Income		20

To record collection of note, with interest, by bank.

Bank Service Charges	10	
Cash		10

To record bank service charges for month of December.

Cash	11	
Accounts Payable		11

To record additional $11 ($66 – $55) when bookkeeper erroneously charged cash account $66 instead of $55.

Accounts Receivable	200	
Cash		200

To record customer's NSF check as an Account Receivable.

Key 34   Petty cash

OVERVIEW *Many businesses find it uneconomical and inconvenient to write a separate check for small items such as stationery, postage, and taxi fares. Therefore, companies keep a small petty cash fund on hand to pay for such expenditures.*

Creating an account: At the time the fund is established, a ledger account called Petty Cash is debited and Cash is credited.

KEY EXAMPLE

The accountant for the Melton Company, a newly formed enterprise, found it necessary to set up a petty cash fund. He therefore drew a check of $100 for the estimated amount and made the following entry:

Petty Cash	100	
Cash		100

To record the establishment of a petty cash fund.

The initial $100 is an estimated amount. It may later be increased or decreased as required by the needs of the business.

Imprest system: Most petty cash funds use an imprest system. Under this system, a fund is established at a fixed amount and the fund is periodically reimbursed, usually at the end of the month, by a single check that equals the total amount paid out for the period.

- Subsequent payments from the petty cash fund are made by the fund's custodian, who prepares a petty cash voucher.
- This voucher shows the date, amount, and purpose of the expenditure.
- As payment is made, each voucher is marked "paid" and an entry is made in the petty cash book.
- The paid voucher is then placed with the balance of the money in the petty cash box.
- Whenever petty cash runs low, the fund must be replenished.

Assume that petty cash expenditures for the month of January were $72.15, representing amounts paid out for telegrams, postage, miscellaneous office expenses, repairs, and tips. The petty cash book would appear as follows:

Petty Cash Book

Date	Explan.	Voucher	Receipts	Payments	Postage	Office Exp.	Misc. Gen. Exp.
Jan. 1	Established	1	$100.00				
4	Postage	2		$10.50	$10.50		
9	Postage	3		42.90	42.90		
12	Office Exp.	5		4.10		$4.10	
15	Telegram	4		6.90			$6.90
20	Office Exp.	6		2.00		2.00	
29	Repairs	7		5.75			5.75
			$100.00	$72.15	$53.40	$6.10	$12.65
	Balance			27.85			
			$100.00	$100.00			
Feb. 1			$27.85				
	Replenishment		$72.15				

The journal entry to replenish the petty cash fund would be as follows:

Postage	53.40	
Office Expense	6.10	
Miscellaneous General Expense	12.65	
Cash		72.15

To replenish petty cash fund.

Theme 8 SHORT-TERM INVESTMENTS

*C*ash is a necessary but low earnings asset. Financial managers must maintain a sufficient cash balance with which to meet current obligations such as accounts payable when they become due. However, a good financial planner will attempt to take excess cash not needed to meet current obligations and invest it in income-producing short-term investments.

INDIVIDUAL KEYS IN THIS THEME

Key 35   Short-term investments defined

OVERVIEW *Short-term investments are current assets. Because they may be sold at any time, they are also called temporary investments or marketable securities. Long-term investments are intended to be held for more than one year and are reported in the investment section of the balance sheet.*

Types of short-term investments: These include debt and equity securities. Debt securities represent a creditor relationship with the enterprise issuing the debt. Debt securities include U.S. government obligations, and corporate and municipal bonds.

Equity securities represent ownership interests such as common and preferred stock. Debt securities, whether short term or long term, are grouped into three separate categories: held-to-maturity, trading, and available-for-sale.

Key 36   Held-to-maturity securities

OVERVIEW   *Held-to-maturity securities are debt securities that a company has the ability and intent to hold to maturity. Held-to-maturity investments are generally classified as noncurrent (long term) assets unless they mature in less than a year from the balance sheet date.*

KEY EXAMPLE

On October 1, 2003, the Johnson Company bought a $50,000 U.S. Treasury bill, due in six months, for $47,600. Johnson's year-end is December 31. The entry to record the purchase of the short-term investment would be as follows:

2003

Oct. 1	Short-Term Investments		
	(held-to-maturity)	47,600	
	Cash		47,600
	To record purchase of a U.S. Treasury bill		
	due in six months (March 31, 2004).		

The entry to record interest earned for the three-month period at year-end would be as follows:

Dec. 31	Short-Term Investments (held-to-maturity)	1,200	
	Interest Income		1,200
	To record interest income earned for		
	three-month period (Oct. 1–Dec. 31).		

After posting the year-end adjusting entry to record the interest earned but not yet paid, the ledger account would appear as follows:

Short-Term Investments (held-to-maturity)		
Oct. 1	47,600	
Dec. 31	1,200	
Balance	48,800	

When the Treasury bill matures on March 31, 2004, the entry would be as follows:

2004

Mar. 31	Cash	50,000	
	Short-Term Investments (held-to-maturity)		48,800
	Interest Income		1,200

Key 37   Trading securities

OVERVIEW *Trading securities are debt securities that management intends to sell in the near future to generate a profit. Thus they are treated as short-term investments and are reported at fair value. Because trading securities are held primarily for sale in the near future, any applicable premium or discount is not amortized.*

KEY EXAMPLE

On December 11, 2003, the Fennel Company bought the following common and preferred stocks:

Betcha Corp. Common Stock	$ 20,000
Harden Corp. Common Stock	60,000
Barley Corp. Preferred Stock	100,000
	$180,000

The entry to record the purchase of the stocks at December 11, 2003, would be as follows:

Dec. 11 Short-Term Investment	180,000	
Cash		180,000

To record purchase of stocks.

Assume further that the fair value of the stocks decreases at the end of the year as follows:

	Cost	Market Value
Betcha Corp. Common Stock	$ 20,000	$ 25,000
Harden Corp. Common Stock	60,000	40,000
Barley Corp. Preferred Stock	100,000	90,000
	$180,000	$155,000

Because the fair value of the short-term investments is $155,000 and less than total cost, an unrealized loss of $25,000 ($180,000 – $155,000) must be recognized. The journal entry at December 31, 2003, would be as follows:

Dec. 31, 2003	Unrealized Loss on		
	Short-Term Investments	25,000	
	Allowance to Reduce Short-Term		
	Investments from Cost to		
	Fair Value		25,000
	To recognize decline in fair value		
	of short-term investments at year-end.		

The loss is reported on the income statement. The allowance account is reported on the balance sheet as follows:

Current Assets

Cash		$100,000
Short-Term Investments (at cost)	$180,000	
Less: Allowance to Adjust Short-Term		
Investments to Fair Value	25,000	155,000

If the fair value of the short-term investment securities increases above cost at year-end, the securities must be shown on the balance sheet at original cost. Assume that on December 31, 2004, a year later, the equity securities have increased in value to $190,000. The allowance account from the prior year would have to be eliminated by recording an unrealized gain equal to the amount of the allowance account set up in the prior year. Note, however, that any increase in value above original total cost cannot be recognized. The journal entry at December 31, 2004, would appear as follows:

Dec. 31, 2004	Allowance to Reduce Short-Term		
	Investments from Cost to		
	Fair Value	25,000	
	Unrealized Gain on		
	Short-Term Investments		25,000
	To eliminate allowance account		
	because fair value exceeds		
	original cost.		

The year-end balance sheet would reflect the total original cost of $180,000 as follows:

Current Assets

Cash	$100,000
Short-Term Investments (at cost)	
(fair value equals $190,000)	180,000

Stocks pay dividends whereas bonds and other types of temporary investments pay interest.

Assume that on February 15, 2004, the short-term investments paid the following cash dividends:

	Cost	Dividends
Betcha Corp. Common Stock	$ 20,000	$2,000
Harden Corp. Common Stock	60,000	1,500
Barley Corp. Preferred Stock	100,000	5,000
	$180,000	$8,500

The journal entry to record the cash dividends received would be recorded as follows:

Feb. 15	Cash	8,500	
	Dividend Income		8,500
	To record receipt of cash dividends.		

The Allowance to Reduce Short-Term Investments from Cost to Market is never changed during the year, even when an investment is sold. Any adjustments must be made only at year-end based upon the entire value of all of the investments.

KEY EXAMPLE

On April 2, 2004, all of the shares of Barley Corp. are sold for $110,000. The entry to record the sale would be as follows:

Apr. 2	Cash	110,000	
	Barley Corp.		100,000
	Realized Gain on Sale of Investments		10,000
	To record sale of Barley preferred stock.		

The gain from the sale would be recorded on the income statement under "Other Income and Expenses."

Key 38   Available-for-sale securities

OVERVIEW *Available-for-sale securities are debt and equity securities that do not fall into either of the above categories.*

Investments in available-for-sale securities are reported at their fair values and any unrealized gains or losses are reported in an unrealized gain or loss account that is part of stockholders' equity. Unrealized gains and losses are not reported in the income statement.

KEY EXAMPLE

On January 1, 2003, Epic Corp. purchases $100,000 of ten-year bonds for $110,000 which results in a bond premium of $10,000. The bonds pay 6% semi-annually on July 1 and January 1. Management has elected to categorize the purchase as available-for-sale securities. The entry to record the purchase of the bonds would be as follows:

Jan. 1	Available-for-Sale Securities	110,000	
	Cash		110,000
	To record purchase of securities.		

At July 1, interest income earned is $3,000 ($100,000 × 6% × six months) and straight line bond premium amortization is $500. The journal entry to record the bond premium amortization and interest income would be as follows:

July 1	Cash	3,000	
	Available-for-Sale Securities		500
	Interest Revenue		2,500
	To record receipt of interest and amortization of bond premium.		

At December 31, interest income accrued is $3,000 ($100,000 × 6% × six months) and straight line bond premium amortization is $500. The journal entry to record the bond premium amortization and interest income would be as follows:

Dec. 31	Interest Receivable	3,000	
	Available-for-Sale Securities		500
	Interest Revenue		2,500
	To set up accrued interest receivable and amortization of bond premium.		

After making the bond premium amortization entries for the year, the balance in the Available-for-Sale Securities account would be $109,000, computed as follows:

Available-for-Sale Securities			
Jan. 1	110,000	July 1	500
		Dec. 31	500
Balance	109,000		1,000

Assume further that at December 31, 2003, the year end fair value of the bonds is $108,000. Thus there is an unrealized holding loss of $1,000 ($109,000 − $108,000) which must be recorded at year-end as follows:

Dec. 31	Unrealized Holding Gain or	1,000
	Loss-Equity	
	Securities Fair Value Adjustment	
	(Available-for-Sale)	1,000
	To record unrealized loss at year-end.	

The loss is reported as a separate component of stockholders' equity and **not recorded in net income**. The balance sheet presentation at December 31, 2003, would appear as follows:

Current assets

Interest Receivable	$ 3,000

Investments

Available-for-Sale Securities (at fair value)	108,000

Stockholders' equity

Unrealized holding loss	Dr. 1,000

Note that the unrealized holding gain or loss would show a debit balance.

Remember that dividend and interest income for all three categories of investments is shown in the "Other Income and Expenses" section of the income statement.

Theme 9 ACCOUNTS AND NOTES RECEIVABLE

*A*ccounts receivable arise from credit sales to customers and are reported on the balance sheet as current assets. Because credit is offered to increase sales, there are often bad debts, which must be charged to an account called the Allowance for Doubtful Accounts. Any accounts receivable subsequently found to be worthless must be written off against the allowance account. A bad debt may also be written off using the direct write-off method. A promissory note is a written promise to pay to the payee a definite sum of money at a future date. Promissory notes that are due and payable in less than a year are current assets.

INDIVIDUAL KEYS IN THIS THEME

Key 39 Accounts receivable

OVERVIEW *Accounts receivable are short-term liquid assets that arise from sales on credit to customers. This type of credit is often called trade credit.*

Accounts receivable: This term is generally used to describe payments due from credit customers arising out of the sale of goods or the performance of services.

- These trade receivables, which are basically short-term current assets, are normally expected to be collected within the current operating cycle.
- Most companies that sell on credit have credit departments whose responsibility it is to approve or refuse credit to individuals or companies.
- The journal entry to record a sale on credit requires a debit to Accounts Receivable and a credit to Sales or Revenue.

KEY EXAMPLE

On February 8, Sudberry's Department Store sold merchandise valued at $1,000 to a customer. A journal entry would be made as follows:

Feb. 8	Accounts Receivable	1,000	
	Sales		1,000
	To record a credit sale of $1,000.		

If the customer makes payment twenty days later, the journal entry to record the receipt of cash would be as follows:

Feb. 28	Cash	1,000	
	Accounts Receivable		1,000
	To record receipt of payment from customer.		

Subsidiary ledger for accounts receivable: Businesses that have many accounts receivable maintain a separate ledger account called a subsidiary accounts receivable ledger. The subsidiary ledger lists each individual purchaser in alphabetical order, and the amount owed by the customer. The total of the individual receivables in the subsidiary ledger must tie in to the total accounts receivable balance found in the general ledger.

Key 40   Worthless accounts receivable

OVERVIEW *Accounts receivable should be reported at their net realizable value, which is the actual amount expected to be realized in cash.*

Doubtful accounts: In order to establish this balance, an Allowance for Doubtful Accounts ledger account is created to offset the trade accounts receivable on the balance sheet.
* This allowance account will reduce the trade receivables to their net realizable value.
* Any accounts receivable subsequently found to be worthless must be written off against this account.

Uncollectible accounts: There are two basic methods for determining the amount of uncollectible receivables at year-end: the *percentage-of-sales method* and the *aging method* (see Key 42).
* Under the percentage-of-sales method, a predetermined percentage is applied to sales in order to set up an estimated balance in the allowance account at year-end.
* Under this method, any prior balance in the allowance account must be ignored.

KEY EXAMPLE

Proton Company has sales of $5,000,000 for the year and December 31 year-end trade accounts receivable of $200,000. Based on prior experience, management has decided that 1% of sales will be uncollectible. The allowance account already has a debit balance of $1,000 remaining from the prior year's allowance. The allowance account must be increased by $50,000 ($5,000,000 × 1%), and Proton will make the following journal entry at year end:

Dec. 31	Uncollectible Accounts Expense	50,000	
	Allowance for Doubtful Accounts		50,000
	To set up allowance account at year-end.		

The Accounts Receivable and Allowance for Doubtful Accounts ledger accounts would appear as follows at year-end:

Accounts Receivable		Allowance for Doubtful Accounts	
Dec. 31 200,000		Old Bal. 1,000	Dec. 31 50,000
			New Bal. 49,000

The allowance account is shown as an *offset,* or *contra* account, to trade accounts receivable in order to arrive at net realizable receivables. The balance sheet at year-end would appear as follows:

Accounts Receivable	$200,000	
Less: Allowance for Doubtful Accounts	49,000	
Net Realizable Value		$151,000

Assume that on January 2 of the following year, an Account Receivable of $2,000 is determined to be uncollectible. The journal entry writing off the uncollectible receivable would be:

Jan. 2 Allowance for Doubtful Accounts	2,000	
Accounts Receivable		2,000
To record write-off of bad debt.		

Key 41 Write-off of an account receivable

OVERVIEW *The write-off entry has no effect on net income because there is no debit to an expense account. The entry has no effect on net realizable receivables because both the Allowance for Doubtful Accounts account and the Accounts Receivable account are part of the net realizable receivables.*

KEY EXAMPLE

The ledger balances in the Accounts Receivable and Allowance for Doubtful Accounts ledger accounts from Key 40 after the posting of the bad debts write-off would appear as follows:

Accounts Receivable		Allowance for Doubtful Accounts	
Dec. 31 200,000	Jan. 2 2,000	Jan. 2 2,000	Dec. 31 49,000
Bal. 198,000			Bal. 47,000

Immediately after the write-off of the bad debt, the balance sheet would appear as follows:

Accounts Receivable	$198,000	
Less: Allowance for Doubtful Accounts	47,000	
Net Realizable Value		$151,000

Key 42   Aging method

OVERVIEW   *Under the aging method, a schedule is set up whereby the receivables are classified into different age categories. Under this procedure, the longer a receivable is outstanding, the greater the probability that the obligation will not be collected.*

Age categories: The oldest outstanding receivables are put into the highest risk categories.
- Under the aging method, a percentage, based on past experience, is applied to each accounts receivable category in order to arrive at a proper allowance at year-end.
- Any prior balance in the allowance account must be taken into account when recording the year-end adjusting entry.

KEY EXAMPLE

On December 31, Lomas Company had trade accounts receivable of $120,000. Management decided to age these accounts in order to set up a proper balance in the Allowance for Doubtful Accounts account at year-end. The company has elected to use the following experience percentages:

Days Outstanding	Percentage
0–30	2
31–60	3
61–90	5
over 90	10

The allowance for doubtful accounts at year-end was determined to be $5,800 computed as follows:

	Total	0–30	31–60	61–90	Over 90
Amount	$120,000	$30,000	$40,000	$20,000	$30,000
Percentage		2%	3%	5%	10%
Estimated Uncollectible	$5,800	$600	$1,200	$1,000	$3,000

Assume that the Allowance account already had a credit balance of $800 in the account based upon a write-off of previous bad debts for the year. The year-end adjusting entry would be as follows:

Dec. 31 Uncollectible Accounts Expense   5,000
                Allowance for Doubtful Accounts   5,000
            To set up allowance account at year-end
            ($5,800 – $800 credit balance).

The balance sheet presentation at year-end would be as follows:

Accounts Receivable   120,000
Less: Allowance for Doubtful Accounts   5,800
      Net Realizable Value   114,200

The Accounts Receivable and Allowance for Doubtful Accounts ledger accounts would appear as follows at year-end:

Accounts Receivable		Allowance for Doubtful Accounts	
Dec. 31 120,000		Old Bal. 800	
		Dec. 31 5,000	
		New Bal. 5,800	

Assume that on January 2 of the following year, an Account Receivable of $1,000 is determined to be uncollectible. The journal entry writing-off the uncollectible receivable would be:

Jan. 2   Allowance for Doubtful Accounts   1,000
                Accounts Receivable   1,000
            To record write-off of bad debt.

Advantage of the aging or allowance method: It properly matches the bad debt expense against revenues.
- The uncollectible accounts expense is estimated and is recorded in the year that the sale is made.
- Although bad debt write-offs rarely equal the allowance for uncollectibles, most accountants still prefer to use the allowance method.

Key 43   Direct write-off method

OVERVIEW *A third approach to writing off an account receivable, called the direct write-off method, does not utilize an allowance account and none appears on the balance sheet. Instead, the worthless receivable is charged off directly to an expense account in the year of uncollectibility.*

Direct write-off method: This method does not match expenses with revenues and therefore violates the matching principle. Its main advantage is that it is simple to use.

KEY EXAMPLE

The Rodrigo Company uses the direct write-off method for recording bad debts. On January 2, an account receivable of $1,500 is determined to be uncollectible. A journal entry writing off the uncollectible receivable would be made as follows:

Jan. 2	Uncollectible Accounts Expense	1,500	
	Accounts Receivable		1,500
	To record write-off of bad debt		
	using the direct write-off method.		

Key 44 Notes receivable

OVERVIEW *A promissory note is a written promise to pay to the payee a definite sum of money, usually with interest, on demand or at a future date. The receipt of promissory notes that are due and payable in less than a year are recorded as notes receivable in the current asset section of the balance sheet.*

Recording: Notes receivable usually arise from the sale of high-value property such as machinery and automobiles. A note has the advantage of producing interest income and represents a stronger legal claim against debtors than an account receivable.
- An interest-bearing note is recorded at its face value.
- The payee, or person or business to whom the short-term note is payable, records a Note Receivable.
- The maker of the short-term note records a Note Payable in the maker's financial records.

Terms: In accounting for promissory notes, several special terms must be remembered. These terms include the following:
- *Duration of the note.* The duration of the note is the length of time between the issuance date and the maturity date of the note. This period may be stated in either days or months and is used to compute interest.
- *Interest and the interest rate.* Interest is the cost of borrowing money. Interest is based upon the principal (face amount) of the note and is usually computed on the basis of a 360-day year (12 months × 30 days per month). The formula for computing interest is

$$\text{Principal} \times \text{Rate of Interest} \times \text{Time} = \text{Interest}$$

- *Maturity date or due date.* The maturity date is the date on which the maturity value of the note (principal and interest) must be paid. In determining the maturity date of a note, the payee must determine the number of days in the months subsequent to the issuance date. The day upon which the note was issued is not counted.

KEY EXAMPLE

The Bradley Company issued a 90-day note dated March 10. The maturity date of the note is June 8 and is determined as follows:

Time Period of Note			90
	March 31		
Issuance Date	10	21	
	April	30	
	May	31	
Total			82
Maturity Date	June		8

- *Maturity value.* The sum of the principal and interest due at the due date of the note.

KEY EXAMPLE

On June 5, the Kendrick Company made a $10,000 sale and received a six-month note bearing interest at a rate of 12% annually. The journal entry to record the receipt of the note would be as follows:

June 5	Note Receivable	10,000	
	Sales		10,000
	To record receipt of 12%, 90-day note.		

When the note is paid on September 3, the following entry must be made:

Sept. 3	Cash	10,300	
	Note Receivable		10,000
	Interest Income		300
	To record receipt of 90-day note		
	with interest computed as follows:		
	$\$10,000 \times 12\% \times 3/12 = \$300$.		

Key 45   Discounting a note receivable

OVERVIEW *Selling a note before maturity is called discounting a note receivable because the payee receives less than the maturity value of the note. The discount (interest) charged by the bank is the price that the payee must pay for receiving the cash earlier than the due date of the note.*

Discounting a note: A company in need of cash may find it necessary to transfer, by endorsement (meaning that the payee signs the back of the note), its notes receivable to a bank.
- The discount charged by the bank is computed on the maturity value of the note.
- The amount of the proceeds paid to the endorser (the original payee) is the maturity value of the note less the discount.

KEY EXAMPLE

On April 10, the Macomber Company receives a 90-day, 12% note receivable for $2,000. On May 5, the company, in need of cash, discounts the note at its bank. The bank charges a discount rate of 14%. The proceeds from the discounted note will be $2,007.92 computed as follows:

Face value of note dated April 10	$2,000.00
Add: Interest on note: $2,000 \times 12\% \times 90$ days	60.00
Maturity value of note due July 9	$2,060.00
Less: Discount period May 5 to July 9…65 days	
Discount on maturity value—65/360 at 14%	52.08
Proceeds of note after discounting	$2,007.92

The journal entry on May 5 to record the discounting of the note, and the proceeds, is as follows:

May 5 Cash	2,007.92	
Note Receivable		2,000.00
Interest Income		7.92

To record discounting of a 12% 90-day
note with 65 days left at 14%

Contingent liability: When a note receivable is sold or discounted at a bank or other financial institution, the seller-endorser remains contingently liable until the maker pays at maturity. The contingent liability assumed by the seller must be disclosed in the notes to the financial statements.

Key 46   Dishonored notes receivable

OVERVIEW *A note is dishonored if the maker does not pay the note at its maturity date.*

Dishonored notes: A note, once dishonored, is no longer negotiable, and a journal entry must be made debiting an Accounts Receivable account and crediting Notes Receivable for the maturity value of the note.

KEY EXAMPLE

On June 1, the Yazoo Company receives a 60-day, 12% note receivable for $10,000. The note was dishonored on July 31, its due date. The journal entry to record the nonpayment of the note would be as follows:

July 31	Accounts Receivable	10,200	
	Notes Receivable		10,000
	Interest Income		200

To record dishonor of note with interest computed as follows:
$10,000 \times 12\% \times 60/360 = \$200$.

Dishonor of a note: In the event that the maker dishonors a discounted note, the payee, who has already received payment of the note and is therefore contingently liable, must make payment to the bank for the maturity value of the note.
*   Upon dishonor, the bank will also add a protest fee to cover the cost of the statement regarding the facts of the dishonor.
*   This fee will ultimately be paid by the maker of the note.

KEY EXAMPLE

On July 1, the Kokomo Company received a $5,000 90-day, 12% note that was discounted at a bank. The note was ultimately dishonored on its due date. The bank charged Kokomo a protest fee of $10. The journal entry to record the nonpayment of the note, and the protest fee, would be as follows:

Sept. 29 Accounts Receivable   5,160
         Cash   5,160
         To record payment of dishonored note
         receivable that had been previously
         discounted.

The total amount of the Account Receivable was computed as follows:

Face value of note dated July 1	$5,000.00
Add: Interest on note: $5,000 \times 12\% \times 90/360$	150.00
Maturity value of note Sept. 29	$5,150.00
Add: Protest fee	10.00
Total amount of Account Receivable	$5,160.00

Theme 10 ACCOUNTING FOR MERCHANDISE INVENTORY

*A*merchandising entity sells merchandise inventory. Inventory is usually the largest current asset on the balance sheet and consists of all goods purchased and held for resale to customers in the ordinary course of business.

Key 47   Merchandising enterprises

OVERVIEW   *A merchandising entity sells merchandise inventory. The amount that a merchandiser earns from selling inventory is called net sales.*

Inventory: Merchandising enterprises purchase merchandise for resale.
- Merchandise inventory, or simply inventory, is usually the largest current asset on the balance sheet and is listed immediately after accounts receivable.
- The inventory consists of all goods purchased and held for resale to customers in the ordinary course of business.

Discount period: Many businesses purchase goods under terms that entitle them to a reduction in price if they pay for the goods within a discount period. Most purchase discounts consist of the terms 1/10, n/30 or 2/10, EOM.
- The term *1/10* means that the purchaser may deduct 1% off the invoice price of the goods if he or she makes payment within 10 days after the invoice date.
- The term *EOM* means that if the payment is not made within the discount period, the entire price is due no later than the end of the month in which the purchase was made.

KEY EXAMPLE

On June 1, the Kent Company purchased goods for $1,000 from the Rosemarie Company. The terms of the purchase were 2/10, n/EOM. Kent paid on June 10. The entry recording the purchase would be as follows:

June 1   Purchases   1,000
            Accounts Payable   1,000
            To record purchase of inventory on account.

The entry to record the payment within the discount period would appear as follows:

June 10 Accounts Payable   1,000
            Cash   980
            Purchase Discounts   20
            To record payment less applicable
            discount of $20 ($1,000 × 2%).

Key 48   Merchandise inventory systems

OVERVIEW *There are two main systems for accounting for merchandise held for resale: periodic and perpetual.*

Periodic: Under the periodic inventory method, no attempt is made on the date of any sale of merchandise to record the cost of the merchandise sold.
- To determine the correct amount of ending inventory under this method, the inventory is actually counted (called a *physical inventory count*) at the end of the month or year.

Perpetual: Under the perpetual inventory method, both the amount of the sale and the cost of the merchandise sold are recorded at the time the sale is made.
- In this manner, the balance in the inventory account is always current.

Key 49 Merchandise inventory on the income statement

OVERVIEW *Merchandise inventory consists of all goods held for sale in the regular course of business.*

Cost: Cost of goods sold is usually the largest single expense on the income statement of a merchandising business. It is composed of merchandise inventory on hand at the beginning of the period plus purchases less ending inventory.

Merchandise inventory: The term *merchandise inventory* is used to designate merchandise held for sale in the normal course of a whole-sale or retail business as well as materials held for manufacturing purposes.
- The cost of goods bought or manufactured is classified as cost of goods sold on the income statement.
- When calculating cost of goods sold, beginning inventory is added to purchases to determine the cost of goods available for sale.
- Cost of goods sold is determined by subtracting ending inventory from the cost of goods available for sale.
- The calculation for determining cost of goods sold is shown in the following example.

KEY EXAMPLE

Popper Company had inventory of $100,000 at the beginning of the year. The company purchased another $400,000 during the year and had ending inventory of $75,000. The cost of goods sold for the year is $425,000 calculated as follows:

Beginning inventory	$100,000
Add: Purchases	400,000
Goods Available for Sale	$500,000
Less: Ending Inventory	75,000
Cost of Goods Sold	$425,000

Ending inventory: The above example illustrates that ending inventory is needed to calculate cost of goods sold.

- It is important to calculate the correct cost of goods sold (an expense) so that a proper matching of costs can be made against the revenue earned for the accounting period.
- When preparing a company's income statement, net sales of merchandise less cost of goods sold equals gross margin or gross profit.
- Operating expenses are subtracted from gross margin to determine a company's net income for the period.

KEY EXAMPLE

Assume that the cost of goods sold is $425,000, that Popper's sales for the year were $750,000, and that the company's operating expenses were $150,000. Popper's net income for the year would be $175,000 calculated as follows:

Sales		$750,000
Less: Cost of Goods Sold		
Beginning Inventory	$100,000	
Add: Purchases	400,000	
Goods Available for Sale	$500,000	
Less: Ending Inventory	75,000	
Cost of Goods Sold		425,000
Gross Margin		$325,000
Less: Operating Expenses		150,000
Net Income		$175,000

The ending inventory of $75,000 automatically becomes the beginning inventory for next year. Ending inventory has the unique characteristic of appearing both on the income statement and the balance sheet at year-end.

Key 50 Ending inventory

OVERVIEW *Ending inventory might include merchan-dise in transit to the company if the purchasing company has title. Shipping terms, which govern when title to goods passes from the buyer to the seller and who must bear the cost of transportation, include F.O.B. (free on board) ship-ping point and F.O.B. destination.*

Ending inventory: This is determined by counting the items on hand, determining the cost of each item, and then multiplying the unit cost by the number of items on hand. Only those items to which the company has title (ownership) may be included in ending inventory.

F.O.B. shipping point: If the incoming goods were shipped F.O.B. (free on board) shipping point, title passed at the point of origin and the buyer must pay the costs of transportation.

F.O.B. destination: If the goods were shipped F.O.B. destination, title does not pass to the buyer until the goods arrive at their destination and the seller bears the costs of transportation.

Key 51   Inventory costing methods

OVERVIEW   *There are four basic methods of recording the cost of ending inventory. The four methods allowed by GAAP are (1) specific unit cost, (2) average cost, (3) first-in, first-out (FIFO) cost, and (4) last-in, first-out (LIFO) cost. Cost is defined as the price paid or the consideration given to acquire an asset.*

KEY DATA

To illustrate the four methods, the following data for the month of December will be used:

Inventory Data, December 31

December	1	Inventory	100 units @ $40	$4,000
	5	Purchased	50 units @ $45	2,250
	20	Purchased	50 units @ $50	2,500
	30	Purchased	50 units @ $60	3,000
Goods Available for Sale			250 units	$11,750
Sales			100 units	
On hand December 31			150 units	

Specific identification method: Under this method, the cost of the goods sold can be identified as coming from specific purchases. If the 100 units sold consisted of the December 5 purchase of 50 units and the December 30 purchase of 50 units, the total cost of the specific units sold under the specific identification method would be $5,250 and the ending inventory would be $6,500 determined as follows:

Inventory, December 31—Specific Identification Method

50 units @ $45	$2,250	Cost of Goods Available	
50 units @ $60	3,000	for Sale	$11,750
100 units at cost of	$5,250	Less: Cost of	5,250
		Goods Sold	
		Ending inventory (150 units)	$6,500

Average cost method: Under the average cost method, the total goods available for sale is divided by the total number of units available for sale. This gives the average cost per unit. The cost of goods sold would be $4,700 and the ending inventory would be $7,050 determined as follows:

Average unit cost: $11,750 ÷ 250 units = $47
Ending inventory: 150 units @ $47 = $7,050

Cost of Goods Available for Sale	$11,750
Less: Ending Inventory	7,050
Cost of Goods Sold (100 units × $47)	$ 4,700

First-in, first-out (FIFO) cost: Under the first-in, first-out (FIFO) cost method, the first goods purchased are treated as the first items to be sold. Under this method, the cost of goods sold would be $4,000 and the ending inventory would be $7,750, determined as follows:

100 units @ $40 $4,000

Cost of Goods Available for Sale	$11,750
Less: Cost of Goods Sold	4,000
Ending Inventory (100 units)	$ 7,750

100 units at cost of $4,000

Last-in, first-out (LIFO) cost: Under the last-in, first out (LIFO) cost method, the last goods purchased are treated as the first items to be sold. Under this method, the ending inventory consists of "old" goods acquired from the earliest purchases of the period. The cost of goods sold would be $5,500 and the ending inventory would be $6,250, determined as follows:

50 units @ $50 $2,500
50 units @ $60   3,000

Cost of Goods Available for Sale	$11,750
Less: Cost of Goods Sold	5,500
Ending Inventory (150 units)	$ 6,250

100 units at cost of $5,500

Key 52   Lower of cost or market

OVERVIEW *The lower of cost or market (LCM) rule requires that ending inventory be reported at the lower of its historical cost or its market value.*

Conservatism: Conservatism means that an accountant should "anticipate no profits, but anticipate all losses."
- As applied to ending inventory, the accountant must reduce the value of the ending inventory if it appears too high.
- If the market value (current replacement cost) is lower than the historical purchase price of the inventory, then the inventory must be written down to reflect its current value.

KEY EXAMPLE

Assume that the Ryder Corporation had sales of $100,000 for a given year. Its beginning inventory was valued at $20,000 and the company made purchases of $30,000. Assume that ending inventory had an original cost basis of $10,000, but that its current replacement cost at year-end was only $9,000. A comparison of the cost method with the lower of cost or market rule (LCM) would result in a $1,000 ($60,000 − $59,000) difference in gross profit calculated as follows:

		Cost		LCM
Sales		$100,000		$100,000
Cost of Goods Sold:				
Beginning Inventory	$20,000		$20,000	
Purchases	30,000		30,000	
	$50,000		$50,000	
Ending Inventory	10,000		9,000	
Cost of Goods Sold		40,000		41,000
Gross Profit		$ 60,000		$ 59,000

Theme 11 PLANT ASSETS, DEPRECIATION, AND INTANGIBLE ASSETS

Depreciation is the systematic allocation of the cost of an asset over its useful life. Depreciation methods include (1) the straight line method, (2) the declining balance method, (3) the sum-of-the-years'-digits method, and (4) the units-of-production method.

INDIVIDUAL KEYS IN THIS THEME

53 Plant, property, and equipment

54 Determining depreciation

55 Straight line depreciation

56 Declining balance depreciation

57 Sum-of-the-years'-digits depreciation

58 Units-of-production method of depreciation

59 Disposal of plant and equipment

60 Intangible assets

61 Depletion

Key 53 Plant, property, and equipment

OVERVIEW *Fixed assets (1) have a useful life of more than one year, (2) are acquired for use by the enterprise, and (3) are not intended for resale to customers.*

Plant, property, and equipment: The term *plant, property, and equipment* includes all tangible assets, including natural resources, that are intended to be used by the enterprise for more than one accounting period.

Capital expenditures: Costs that benefit more than one period are said to be a capital expenditure and include the purchase price of the fixed asset plus all subsequent costs applicable that are necessary to place the asset into operation.
- The acquisition of a tangible asset is recorded at cost and includes all other expenditures necessary to obtain title to the property and to get it ready for operating use.
- These expenditures may include freight and handling charges, installation costs, insurance, assembly costs, and the cost of running trial tests.
- Daily operating expenses are expensed, not capitalized.

KEY EXAMPLE

On January 2, the Guastella Company purchased, for cash, a machine for $10,000 with freight charges to be paid by the buyer. On January 8, a freight bill of $400 pertaining to the machine was paid by the company. The journal entries to record the acquisition costs applicable to the machine are as follows:

Jan. 2	Machinery	10,000	
	Cash		10,000
	To record purchase of machine.		
Jan. 8	Machinery	400	
	Cash		400
	To record payment of freight charges.		

The ledger account for Machinery, after posting the above entries, would appear as follows:

Machinery

Jan. 2	10,000	
8	400	
	10,400	

Cost of land: All expenditures made to acquire land and to ready it for use by the business is treated as part of the cost of the land. These costs, which must be capitalized, include the purchase price of the land, legal and recording fees, and the cost of clearing and grading the land.

Key 54   Determining depreciation

OVERVIEW *Depreciation is the systematic allocation of the cost of an asset over its estimated useful life. If the fixed assets (property, plant, and equipment) appreciate in value, they should not be written up to reflect market values that are above original cost.*

Depreciation: The basis for an asset's depreciation is its cost. Depreciation methods include (1) the straight line method, (2) the declining balance method, (3) the sum-of-the-years'-digits method, and (4) the units-of-production method (sometimes referred to as the activity method).

- The straight line, sum-of-the-years'-digits, and the units-of-production methods must take into account the salvage value (or residual value) of the asset.
- The declining balance method, unlike the other methods, does not take salvage value into account.
- Salvage value is the estimated amount that is expected to be received when the asset is eventually sold at the end of its useful life.

Key 55 Straight line depreciation

OVERVIEW *Under the straight line method of depreciation, equal periodic charges for depreciation are made to income until the asset is fully depreciated.*

KEY EXAMPLE

Hexagon Company bought a $10,000 machine on January 1. The asset had a useful life of five years, and salvage value at the end of this period was estimated at $1,000. Depreciation for the first year, and for each of the following four years, would be $1,800, computed as follows:

$$\frac{\text{Cost of asset less salvage value }(\$10,000 - \$1,000)}{\text{Estimated life}} \quad \frac{\$9,000}{5 \text{ years}} = \$1,800$$

Once the amount of annual depreciation has been determined, a year-end adjusting entry must be made debiting an expense account called Depreciation Expense and crediting an account called Accumulated Depreciation (sometimes called a contra-asset account). The cost of a depreciable asset, less its applicable accumulated depreciation, is known as its net book value. The journal entry to record the $1,800 of annual depreciation would be as follows:

Dec. 31	Depreciation Expense	1,800	
	Accumulated Depreciation		1,800
	To record depreciation for year.		

The fixed asset section of Hexagon's balance sheet would appear as follows at year-end:

Plant Assets		
Machinery	$10,000	
Less: Accumulated Depreciation	1,800	
Net Book Value		$8,200

Key 56 Declining balance depreciation

OVERVIEW *The declining balance method is an accelerated form of depreciation, which results in larger depreciation charges during the earlier years of an asset's life and smaller charges in the later years. The usual method is to take twice the straight line depreciation rate (called double-declining balance) and apply it to the asset's remaining book value after deducting all prior depreciation. Under this method, estimated salvage value is ignored.*

KEY EXAMPLE

Hexagon elects to use the double-declining balance method of depreciation. The five-year life equals an annual depreciation rate of 20%, which is then doubled to 40%. Therefore, the annual depreciation for years one and two would be $4,000 and $2,400 respectively, computed as follows:

Year	Annual Depreciation Calculation	Annual Depreciation Expense
1	40% × $10,000	$4,000
2	40% × $6,000*	2,400

*$10,000 – $4,000 (depreciation) = $6,000

The journal entry to record the $4,000 of annual depreciation in the first year would be as follows:

Dec. 31	Depreciation Expense	4,000	
	Accumulated Depreciation		4,000
	To record depreciation for the year.		

Key 57   Sum-of-the-years'-digits depreciation

OVERVIEW *Under the sum-of-the-years'-digits method, the years of the asset's service life are added together. This sum becomes the denominator of a series of fractions, which is then applied to the cost of the asset less its salvage value.*

KEY EXAMPLE

Using the facts in Key 55, the denominator would be calculated as follows:

$$1 + 2 + 3 + 4 + 5 = 15 \text{ (denominator)}$$

The annual depreciation schedule for the first three years would then appear as follows:

Year	Annual Depreciation Calculation	Annual Depreciation Expense
1	5/15 × $9,000	$3,000
2	4/15 × 9,000	2,400
3	3/15 × 9,000	1,800

Key 58 Units-of-production method of depreciation

OVERVIEW *Under the units-of-production method, the depreciation rate per year is based upon the production capacity of the asset, such as hours of usage, miles driven, or number of units produced.*

KEY EXAMPLE

Using the facts in Key 55, assume that the machine is expected to produce 90,000 units over its productive life. If the machine produces 10,000 units during its first year of use, the annual depreciation would be $1,000, calculated as follows:

Cost – salvage value = production cost per unit

Estimated units of useful life
$$\frac{\$10,000 - \$1,000}{90,000 \text{ units}} = \$.10 \text{ per unit}$$

Depreciation Expense: 10,000 units produced @ $.10 = $1,000.

Key 59   Disposal of plant and equipment

OVERVIEW *When an asset is sold or discarded, an entry must be made debiting the Accumulated Depreciation Account, crediting the appropriate asset account, and recording a loss, if there is any remaining undepreciated value to book asset.*

KEY EXAMPLE 1

On December 31, the Vorgate Company disposed of a machine that had an original cost of $10,000 and was fully depreciated at the time of its disposal. The journal entry to record the disposal would be as follows:

Dec. 31	Accumulated Depreciation	10,000	
	Machine		10,000
	To record disposal of asset.		

KEY EXAMPLE 2

On July 1, the Mechano Company disposed of a partially depreciated asset that had an original cost basis of $20,000 and $18,000 in accumulated depreciation at the end of the previous year. Assuming that Mechano was using straight line depreciation over a ten-year life and there was no salvage value, the journal entries at July 1 to record the updating of depreciation for six months and the subsequent disposal of the asset would be made as follows:

July 1	Depreciation Expense	1,000	
	Accumulated Depreciation		1,000
	$20,000 cost ÷ 10 years = $2,000		
	× 6/12 = $1,000		
July 1	Accumulated Depreciation	19,000	
	Loss on Disposal of Plant Asset	1,000	
	Machine		20,000
	To record disposal of plant asset.		

The account Loss on Disposal of Plant Asset would be closed out into Income Summary at year-end.

The account Gain on Sale of Plant Asset would be closed out into Income Summary at year-end.

Key 60 Intangible assets

OVERVIEW *Intangible assets consist of noncurrent assets that have no physical substance.*

Intangible assets: These assets, which include goodwill, patents, copyrights, trademarks, trade names, and computer software development costs, are usually valued at their cost.
* Goodwill is recorded only when one business purchases another for an amount in excess of the fair market value of the net assets of the company acquired.
* If there is no excess cost, then goodwill cannot be recorded.

Amortization of intangibles: Most intangible assets, such as patents, have a definite legal life and must, therefore, be amortized over their useful (or economic) life.
* Intangible assets are amortized using the straight line basis of amortization.
* Where the life of an intangible asset is indefinite, it must be amortized over a reasonable period of time, not to exceed 40 years.
* Some intangible assets, such as patents, have a limited legal life of 20 years from the date the patent application is filed.

KEY EXAMPLE

On January 1, the Belko Company purchased a patent for $20,000. The entry to record amortization of the patent at year-end would be as follows:

Dec. 31 Amortization Expense (Patent)   1,000
        Patent   1,000
        To record annual amortization:
        $20,000 ÷ 20 years = $1,000.

Loss: Intangible assets that are determined to be worthless must be written off as a loss.

Key 61 Depletion

OVERVIEW *Wasting assets, such as oil wells, copper deposits, or timber, are subject to depletion.*

Depletion: Periodic depletion is calculated according to the "units-of-production" method, whereby a charge to depletion is made for each mineral unit mined and sold.

KEY EXAMPLE

Zoltan Industries purchased for $1,000,000 a mineral deposit estimated to contain 1,000,000 tons of coal. During its first year of operation, Zoltan mined 200,000 tons of coal and sold 150,000 tons. The depletion rate per unit would be $1.00, and the year-end charge for depletion would be $150,000 calculated as follows:

Depletion per ton:

$$\frac{\text{Cost of mineral deposit}}{\text{Estimated tonnage in deposits}} \quad \frac{\$1,000,000}{1,000,000} = \$1 \text{ per ton}$$

150,000 tons sold × $1 = $150,000 annual depletion.

The journal entry to record the annual depletion would be:

Dec. 31 Depletion Expense   150,000
        Accumulated Depletion   150,000
        To record depletion based upon the units sold.

Basis: Depletion cost is based on the units sold and not on those mined.
- The unsold units are treated as ending inventory and appear on the balance sheet.
- The accumulated depletion account appears as a contra asset account and is presented in the balance sheet as a deduction from the cost of the mineral deposit.

Theme 12 LIABILITIES

*C*urrent liabilities represent obligations maturing within one year of the balance sheet date or within the operating cycle, whichever is longer. Examples include accounts and notes payable and withholding taxes payable. Long-term liabilities are those that, by their terms, mature more than one year after the date of the financial statements. Examples include bonds payable and mortgage notes payable.

Key 62   Current liabilities

OVERVIEW *Current liabilities represent obligations maturing within one year of the balance sheet date or within the operating cycle, whichever is longer. Current liabilities are paid out of current assets such as cash.*

Accounts payable: Amounts owed for goods and services purchased by the enterprise on account. Accounts payable, as well as similar obligations, should be reflected on the year-end balance sheet.

KEY EXAMPLE

On January 2, the Buxton Company hired Window Washers Inc. to clean their windows. Upon completion of the job, Window Washers mailed Buxton a bill for $100, payable on February 1. The entry to record the amount owed to Window Washers (a current liability) would be recorded as follows:

Jan. 2	Office Cleaning and Maintenance	100	
	Accounts Payable		100
	To record liability for services		
	rendered to Buxton.		

When the account payable is paid on February 1, the journal entry would be as follows:

Feb. 1	Accounts Payable	100	
	Cash		100
	To record payment of liability.		

Subsidiary ledger for accounts payable: Businesses that have many accounts payable maintain a separate ledger account called a subsidiary accounts payable ledger. The subsidiary ledger lists each individual seller of goods and services, in alphabetical order, and the amount owed to each vendor. The total of the individual payables in the subsidiary ledger must tie in to the total accounts payable balance found in the general ledger.

Key 63 Merchandise bought on account

OVERVIEW *Merchandise purchased by an entity is usually bought on account under F.O.B. shipping point or F.O.B. destination terms.*

F.O.B. shipping point: If merchandise purchased by an entity were bought on account under F.O.B. (free on board) terms, the goods are inventoriable when shipped and a corresponding liability should be recorded at the same time.

F.O.B. destination: Where the goods are shipped under a destination contract (F.O.B. destination), title will not pass until the goods arrive. Therefore, no liability should be recorded until the goods are received.

KEY EXAMPLE

On December 27, the O'Sullivan Company purchased $100,000 of inventory for resale. The shipping terms were F.O.B. shipping point, n/EOM (end of month). The goods were shipped the same day, but were not received until January 3 of the following year. Since the entity bought the goods on account under F.O.B. (free on board) terms, the goods are inventoriable when shipped and a corresponding liability should be recorded at the same time. The entry to record the amount owed to O'Sullivan (a current liability) would be recorded as follows:

Dec. 27 Purchases	100,000	
Accounts Payable		100,000
To record purchase of merchandise, terms n/EOM.		

Key 64 Notes payable

OVERVIEW *Notes payable are written promissory notes that arise out of the ordinary course of business. Notes are usually issued to suppliers for goods and services delivered and to banks for loans.*

KEY EXAMPLE

On July 1, the Patrick Company borrowed $10,000 from the Amalgamated Trust Company by issuing a 30-day, 12% promissory note.

July 1	Cash	10,000	
	Notes Payable		10,000
	To record issuance of 30-day,		
	12% promissory note.		

When the note is paid on July 31, the journal entry would appear as follows:

July 31	Notes Payable	10,000	
	Interest Expense	100	
	Cash		10,100
	To record payment of 30-day, 12%		
	promissory note with interest calculated		
	as follows: $10,000 \times 30/360 \times 12\% = \$100$		
	note with interest.		

Key 65 Advance payments from customers

OVERVIEW *When monies for goods and services are received in advance of the delivery date, a liability is created. Examples: magazine subscriptions, passenger revenues, meal tickets, and tuition payments.*

When income is earned: Income from these items is considered to be earned only at the time the goods are furnished or the services are provided.
- Unearned amounts are treated as current liabilities on the balance sheet at year-end.
- When the merchandise is delivered or the service is performed, the amounts are considered to be earned and are transferred from a liability to a revenue account.

KEY EXAMPLE

On December 1, the Wentworth Publishing Company received $12,000 in prepaid one-year magazine subscriptions. The entry to record the unearned subscriptions (a current liability) would be recorded as follows:

Dec. 1	Cash	12,000	
	Unearned Subscription Income		12,000
	To record unearned subscription income for twelve-month period.		

At the end of December, one month of magazine subscriptions has been earned. The amount of $1,000 is considered to be earned and must be transferred from the liability to the revenue account as follows:

Dec. 31	Unearned Subscription Income	1,000	
	Subscription Income		1,000
	To record one month of the prepaid subscriptions income earned.		

Key 66   Taxes and other payroll
deductions

OVERVIEW *The most common types of current liabilities in this category include federal, state, and city payroll withholding taxes. Other payroll deductions include medical insurance premiums, employee savings, and union dues.*

KEY EXAMPLE

Murtha Company's weekly payroll is $10,000. Employee withholding amounts include the following: federal income taxes, $2,000; Social Security taxes, $765, and a medical insurance premium, $1,000. The journal entry required to record the payroll expense and liability would be as follows:

Salary Expense	10,000	
Federal Withholding Taxes Payable		2,000
Social Security Taxes Payable		765
Medical Insurance Premiums Payable		1,000
Cash		6,235
To record liability for payroll.		

Key 67 Noncurrent liabilities

OVERVIEW *Long-term liability is debt that, by its terms, matures more than one year after the date of the financial statements.*

Bonds as long-term debt: Bonds represent money borrowed by a corporation and are sold to the investing public. A sale of a bond should not be confused with the sale of corporate stocks. Bondholders are actually creditors who expect to earn interest from the bonds. Stockholders are the owners of the corporation and expect to receive dividends.

Bonds as borrowing: The board of directors of a corporation votes a bond issue. This issue might consist of a $10,000,000 issue consisting of a thousand $10,000 bonds.
   • The agreement between the corporation and the bondholders defining the rights of the bondholders is called a bond indenture.
   • The bond indenture usually describes such things as the maturity date of the bonds, the rate of interest that the bonds will pay, the interest payment dates, and whether or not a bond sinking fund will be created to pay the bonds at maturity.
   • The corporation will also select a trustee to represent the interests of the bondholders. The trustee is generally a large bank.

Types of bonds: The most common types of bonds are registered and coupon bonds.
   • A registered bond is issued in the bondholder's name and interest is paid directly to the bondholder.
   • A coupon bond is generally payable to bearer and interest is payable to the individual who presents the interest coupon for payment.
   • Mortgage bonds are secured by the assets of the corporation selling the bonds.
   • A bond unsecured by any corporate assets but issued by a financially sound corporation is called a debenture bond.
   • Callable bonds permit an issuing corporation to redeem the bonds at any time prior to their maturity date by paying a specified price.

Key 68   Accounting for the sale of bonds

OVERVIEW   *Bonds may be issued at their face amount (also called par value), above par value (at a premium), or below par (at a discount).*

Price: Bonds are quoted as a percentage of their face value or maturity date. The maturity value is the amount the issuing company must pay to redeem the bonds. Thus, a $1,000 bond quoted at 95 would have a market price of $950 ($1,000 × 95).

Accounting: When a bond issue is sold, cash is debited and a long-term liability called bonds payable is credited.

KEY EXAMPLE

On December 31, 2002, the Oglethorpe Corporation issued $10 million worth of 10-year bonds at 9% at par value due on January 1, 2013. The journal entry to record the sale of the bonds would be as follows:

Dec. 31	Cash	10,000,000
	Bonds Payable	10,000,000
	To record sale of 9% ten-year bonds	
	at their face.	

Bonds, as long-term debt, appears on Oglethorpe's balance sheet at December 31, 2002, as follows:

Long-Term Liabilities
Bonds Payable (9%) due December 31, 2013 10,000,000

If the bonds paid interest at a rate of 9% annually, and the bond indenture agreement required the payments to be made at six-month intervals (called semiannual payments), the journal entry recording the payment of interest at July 1, 2003, the following year, would be as follows:

July 1	Interest Expense	450,000
	Cash	450,000
	To record payment of interest for six-	
	month period: (Jan. 1, 2003 to June 30, 2003)	
	$10,000,000 × 9% × 6/12 = $450,000.	

The next interest payment of $450,000 would be on January 1, 2004.

Key 69   Sale of bonds at a premium

OVERVIEW *Bonds will sell at a premium if the interest rate paid by the bonds is above the market rate. This premium must be amortized over the life of the bond.*

Premium: Bonds are sold at a premium because the rate of interest that the bond is paying is more than investors would receive on other investments made at the current market rate. Because of this higher rate of return, investors are willing to pay more for the bond.
* The premium must be amortized over the life of the bond and, therefore, a reduction of interest expense.
* Many companies use the straight line method of amortization although another method, called the effective interest method, is sometimes used.

KEY EXAMPLE

Assume the same facts as in Key 68, except that the bonds are sold on December 31, 2002, at 102. The entry to record the sale of the bonds at a premium would be as follows:

Dec. 31	Cash	10,200,000	
	Bonds Payable		10,000,000
	Premium on bonds payable		200,000
	To record sale of bonds at a price of 102.		

Bonds, as long-term debt, appear on Oglethorpe's balance sheet at December 31, 2002, as follows:

Long-Term Liabilities
Bonds Payable (9%) due January 1, 2013 $10,000,000
Add: Premium on Bonds Payable   200,000 $10,200,000

If the bonds paid interest at a rate of 9% annually, and the bond indenture agreement required the payments to be made at six-month intervals (called semiannual payments), the journal entry recording the payment of interest at July 1, 2003, the following year, would be as follows:

July 1	Interest Expense	450,000	
	Cash		450,000

To record payment of interest for six-month period: (Jan. 1, 2003 to June 20, 2003) $10,000,000 \times 9\% \times 6/12 = \$450,000$.

The next interest payment of $450,000 would be on January 1, 2004.

Key 70   Sale of bonds at a discount

OVERVIEW   *Bonds will sell at a discount if the interest rate paid by the bonds is below the market rate. This discount must be amortized over the life of the bond.*

Discount: Bonds are sold at a discount because the rate of interest that the bond is paying is less than investors would receive on other investments made at the current market rate. Because of this lower rate of return, investors are not willing to pay par value for the bond.
- The discount must be amortized over the life of the bond and therefore an increase of interest expense.
- Many companies use the straight line method of amortization, although another method, called the effective interest method, is sometimes used.

KEY EXAMPLE

Assume the same facts as in Key 68, except that the bonds are sold on December 31, 2002, at 98. The entry to record the sale of the bonds at a discount would be as follows:

Dec. 31	Cash	9,800,000	
	Discount on Bonds Payable	200,000	
	Bonds Payable		10,000,000
	To record sale of bonds at a price of 98.		

Bonds, as long-term debt, appear on Oglethorpe's balance sheet at December 31, 2002, as follows:

Long-Term Liabilities		
Bonds Payable (9%) due January 1, 2013	$10,000,000	
Less: Discount on Bonds Payable	200,000	$9,800,000

If the bonds paid interest at a rate of 9% annually, and the bond indenture agreement required the payments to be made at six-month intervals, the journal entry recording the payment of interest at July 1, 2003, the following year, would be as follows:

July 1	Interest Expense	450,000	
	Cash		450,000

To record payment of interest for six-month period: (Jan. 1, 2003 to June 20, 2003) $10,000,000 \times 9\% \times 6/12 = \$450,000$.

The next interest payment of $450,000 on the bonds would be on January 1, 2004.

Key 71 Repayment of bonds payable at maturity

OVERVIEW *Outstanding bonds are repaid or retired at their maturity date. Even if the bonds were originally issued at a premium or a discount, the entry made debits bonds payable and credits cash.*

Recording retirement of a bond: All outstanding bonds are eventually retired, either at their maturity date or, if they are callable, at a specified price prior to their maturity.
- The specified price is usually slightly above the face value of the bonds.
- If the bonds that were sold at either a premium or a discount are held to their maturity, there would be no balance in either the premium or discount accounts since these accounts would have been fully amortized over the life of the bonds.

KEY EXAMPLE

Assume that Oglethorpe's outstanding bonds are repaid on December 31, 2012. The entry to record the repayment of the bonds would be as follows:

Dec. 31	Bonds Payable	10,000,000	
	Cash		10,000,000
	To record retirement of bonds.		

Key 72   Mortgage notes payable

OVERVIEW *The common form of long-term notes payable is a mortgage note payable.*

Mortgage notes payable: On the balance sheet, the liability should be reported as a "Mortgage Note Payable" together with a brief footnote stating that the note is secured by certain property.

KEY EXAMPLE

On February 1, the Connor Corporation borrowed $5,000,000 from the Royal Bank with a stated rate of interest of 8%. As security in case of nonpayment of the loan, the corporation pledged its office building.

Feb. 1	Cash	5,000,000	
	Mortgage Note Payable		5,000,000
	To record mortgage note payable		
	issued to the Royal Bank for loan.		

A footnote in the financial statements would indicate that the loan is secured by a title to its office building.

Theme 13 PARTNERSHIPS

*I*n a partnership, two or more persons carry on as co-owners of a business for profit. Assets are usually contributed by the partners and are recorded by the partnership at their fair market values. Profits are divided up according to the partnership agreement. A partnership may eventually decide to terminate operations and liquidate its assets. The sale of these partnership assets is called realization.

INDIVIDUAL KEYS IN THIS THEME

Key 73   Definition of a partnership

OVERVIEW *The Uniform Partnership Act, which has been adopted by virtually all states, defines a partnership as "an association of two or more persons to carry on as co-workers of a business for profit."*

Articles of partnership: Most partnerships are formed through an agreement between the participants, known as the articles of partnership.
- This document states, among its many provisions, the name, location, and purposes of the business, how much each partner is to invest in the enterprise, how much each partner is to take out of the business by way of withdrawals, how profits are to be distributed, and the procedures for terminating the partnership.
- This agreement is legally binding on all of the partners.

Uniform Partnership Act: Besides the partnership agreement, the Uniform Partnership Act (UPA) imposes certain rules that will affect the operation of the partnership. Example: The UPA states that a partnership will automatically terminate if a partner becomes bankrupt, dies, or sells his interest.

Liability: Like the sole proprietorship, the partnership arrangement carries unlimited liability for the owners. Although the partnership offers the advantage of sharing profits and losses, it also presents the problem of the wealthier owners absorbing a greater share of the losses if the poorer partners cannot.

Key 74   Partners' equity

OVERVIEW *All assets contributed to the partnership are recorded by the partnership at their fair market values. All liabilities applicable to those assets are also recorded.*

Accounting: For the assets and liabilities of a newly formed partnership, the accounting is similar to that of a sole proprietorship. The major difference is that owners' equity is called partners' equity and each partner must maintain a separate withdrawal and capital account.

- All assets contributed by the partners, including noncash assets, such as land and buildings, must be recorded at their fair market values.

KEY EXAMPLE

Peter Elroy and Lena Avis form a partnership. Elroy agrees to transfer the following assets and liabilities to the partnership as his investment: Cash $8,000; Accounts Receivable $28,000; Allowance for Doubtful Accounts $2,800; Equipment costing $40,000; Accumulated Depreciation $12,000; Accounts Payable $4,000; and Notes Payable $2,000. The equipment is worth only $20,000. Avis agrees to invest $50,000 in cash. The journal entries recording their initial investments would be as follows:

Cash	8,000	
Accounts Receivable	28,000	
Equipment	20,000	
Allowance for Doubtful Accounts		2,800
Accounts Payable		4,000
Notes Payable		2,000
Peter Elroy, Capital		47,200

To record initial investment of Peter Elroy.

Cash	50,000	
Lena Avis, Capital		50,000

To record initial investment of Lena Avis.

At this point, the partners' equity section of the balance sheet would list the balance in each partner's account separately, as shown in the following partial balance sheet:

Liabilities and Partners' Equity

Total Liabilities		$6,000
Partners' Equity		
Elroy, Capital	$47,200	
Avis, Capital	50,000	
Total Partners' Equity		97,200
Total Liabilities and Partners' Equity		$103,200

Key 75   Division of profits and losses

OVERVIEW *The capital account is an equity (meaning ownership) account similar to the shareholder's equity accounts in a corporation. It is used to account for withdrawals, additional contributions by each partner, and net income or loss.*

Profit: The method of dividing up profit to be used in any given situation is usually found in the partnership agreement.
- If the agreement does not specify how profits and losses are to be shared, the UPA requires that profits and losses be divided equally.

Losses: If the agreement specifies how profits are to be shared but says nothing about losses, then losses are to be shared in the same manner as profits.
- The ratio of sharing profits and losses can be totally independent of the partners' ownerships interests. Example: In Key 74, Elroy and Avis, who have an almost equal amount invested in the partnership, can agree to share profits and losses in a ratio of 70% and 30% respectively.

KEY EXAMPLE

Zane and Fitz form a partnership with an investment of $40,000 and $20,000 respectively. If their partnership agreement says nothing about the division of profits and their Income Summary account shows a profit of $48,000 at year end, the journal entry to record the distribution of profits at December 31 would be as follows:

Dec. 31 Income Summary	48,000	
Zane, Capital		24,000
Fitz, Capital		24,000
To distribute the income equally		
for the year to the partners' capital		
accounts.		

Assume the same facts, except that the partners agree to share profits in the ratio of 3:1.

Dec. 31	Income Summary	48,000	
	Zane, Capital		36,000
	Fitz, Capital		12,000

To distribute the income for the year
to the partners' capital accounts as
follows:

Zane (3/4) × $48,000 = $36,000
Fitz (1/4) × $48,000 =   12,000
                        $48,000

Key 76 Additional investments, division of profits, closing entries, and capital statement

OVERVIEW *A partnership may require an additional cash investment after it begins operations. These additional contributions are credited to the capital accounts of each contributing partner. On the other hand, withdrawals represent cash payments to partners for personal living expenses.*

KEY EXAMPLE

A portion of the ledger accounts for the Wonder Partnership, after all revenue and expense accounts have been closed into Income Summary, is presented as follows:

Cooper, Capital	
	1/1 40,000
	6/1 8,000

Crane, Capital	
	1/1 60,000
	4/1 20,000
	8/1 12,000

Cooper, Withdrawals	
20,000	

Crane, Withdrawals	
14,000	

Income Summary	
	50,000

Their profit-sharing agreement provides for interest at 10% on initial capital balances, salaries of $24,000 for Cooper and $12,000 for Crane, and the remainder to be divided equally. Based upon the above information, the following year-end closing entries would be made as follows:

Dec. 31	Income Summary	50,000	
	Cooper, Capital		30,000
	Crane, Capital		20,000
	To record distribution of profits according		
	to a predetermined formula per the partnership		
	agreement calculated as follows:		

	Cooper	Crane	Total
Interest at 10%			
Cooper 10% × $40,000	$4,000		$4,000
Crane 10% × $60,000		$6,000	6,000
Salaries	24,000	12,000	36,000
Remainder Equally	2,000	2,000	4,000
	$30,000	$20,000	$50,000

The closing entries for the withdrawal accounts would appear as follows at year-end:

Dec. 31	Cooper, Capital	20,000	
	Cooper, Withdrawals		20,000
	To close withdrawal account into capital.		
Dec. 31	Crane, Capital	14,000	
	Crane, Withdrawals		14,000
	To close withdrawal account into capital.		

A summary of each partner's capital account after the distribution of profits, and the closing of the withdrawal accounts into capital, would appear as follows:

	Cooper	Crane	Total
Capital, January 1	$40,000	$60,000	$100,000
Additional Investments During the Year	8,000	32,000	40,000
	$48,000	$92,000	$140,000
Net Income for Year	30,000	20,000	50,000
	$78,000	$112,000	$190,000
Less: Withdrawals During Year	20,000	14,000	34,000
Capital, December 31	$58,000	$98,000	$156,000

The partner's equity section of the balance sheet would list the balance in each partner's account separately, as follows:

Partners' Equity
Cooper, Capital	$58,000	
Crane, Capital	98,000	
Total Partners' Equity		$156,000

Key 77 Admission of a new partner

OVERVIEW *An individual may become a partner in an existing partnership only with the unanimous consent of the current partners. A new partner can be admitted by either purchasing the interest of an existing partner or by contributing assets such as cash or equipment.*

Admission by purchasing an interest: The admission of a new partner will dissolve the old partnership because a new association of individuals has been formed.
- A new partner can be admitted by purchasing an interest from an old partner.
- The transaction is considered a personal arrangement between the two individuals.
- The journal entry recording the change in ownership will reflect the book value of the interest and not the amount of cash that changed hands.

KEY EXAMPLE

On July 1, Jose Velez sold his $80,000 interest in a partnership to Allen Green for $100,000. The journal entry on the partnership books that records the sale would appear as follows:

July 1	Jose Velez, Capital	80,000	
	Allen Green, Capital		80,000
	To record the transfer of Velez's		
	partnership interest to Green.		

In the above transaction the book value of $80,000 is recorded and not the purchase price of $100,000.

Attributing goodwill to the old partnership: Sometimes a new partner is admitted after recording goodwill attributable to the old partnership.
- Goodwill is an intangible asset generated by an existing business based upon the quality of its product, the integrity of its management, the number of years in business, and its location.

KEY EXAMPLE

On April 1, the partnership of Jane Kringle and Lulu Jasper agree to admit Clark Williams for $30,000. Williams is to receive a one-third interest. The capital account balances of Kringle and Jasper are $28,000 and $23,000 respectively. They agree that prior to the admission of Williams, the enterprise is worth $60,000. The excess of $60,000 over the capital balances of $51,000 ($28,000 + $23,000) indicates the existence of $9,000 in goodwill. If the partnership agreement stipulates that profits and losses are to be shared equally, the journal entry to record the goodwill prior to the admission of Williams, and the $30,000 investment by Williams, would be as follows:

April 1	Goodwill	9,000	
	Jane Kringle, Capital		4,500
	Lulu Jasper, Capital		4,500
	To record goodwill on the partnership books prior to the admission of Clark Williams.		
April 1	Cash	30,000	
	Clark Williams, Capital		30,000
	To record the investment of Clark Williams for an interest in the partnership.		

The partners' equity section of the balance sheet would list the balance in each partner's account after the transaction would appear as follows:

Partners' Equity		
Kringle, Capital	$32,500	
Jasper, Capital	27,500	
Williams, Capital	30,000	
Total Partners' Equity		$90,000

Key 78 Liquidation of a partnership

OVERVIEW *Liquidation is the process whereby a partnership elects to go out of business by selling its assets, paying its creditors, and distributing the remaining cash to the partners according to their respective claims.*

Termination of the partnership: A partnership may eventually decide to terminate operations and liquidate its assets.
- The sale of these partnership assets is called realization. Under this procedure, the assets are sold at either a gain or a loss.
- Any gain or loss is then distributed among the partnership capital accounts in accordance with the partnership agreement.
- Once the cash from the sale of all the assets is realized, creditors are paid off and any remaining cash is distributed to the partners in accordance with the remaining balances in their respective capital accounts.

KEY EXAMPLE

Tom Miles, Roy Binns, and Fay Salt are partners with a profit-sharing agreement of 1:2:2. On May 1, after closing the accounts in anticipation of liquidating their partnership, the following trial balance was taken:

Cash	$ 3,600	
Accounts Receivable	22,000	
Merchandise Inventory	28,000	
Equipment	24,000	
Accumulated Depreciation		$14,000
Accounts Payable		16,000
Tom Miles, Capital		20,000
Roy Binns, Capital		18,000
Fay Salt, Capital		9,600
	$77,600	$77,600

Accounting for the sale of assets: The accounts receivable were sold for $18,000 and the merchandise inventory was sold at auction for $16,500. The equipment was deemed worthless and scrapped.
- If any partner's capital account was unable to absorb any loss that was caused by the disposal of the assets, the loss was to be shared by the remaining partners.

The journal entries on May 1 recording the cash realized from the sale of the assets and steps taken in the eventual liquidation of the partnership are as follows:

May 1	Cash	18,000	
	Loss on Disposal of Assets	4,000	
	Accounts Receivable		22,000
	To record sale of receivables		
	at a $4,000 loss.		
May 1	Cash	16,500	
	Loss on Disposal of Assets	11,500	
	Merchandise Inventory		28,000
	To record sale of inventory		
	at a $11,500 loss.		
May 1	Accumulated Depreciation	14,000	
	Loss on Disposal of Assets	10,000	
	Equipment		24,000
	To record loss due to scrapping		
	of equipment.		

At this point, the ledger account Loss on Disposal of Assets, after all applicable postings, would appear as follows:

Loss on Disposal of Assets

May 1	4,000	
	11,500	
	10,000	
	25,500	

The journal entry to record the absorption of the total loss in the account would be as follows:

May 1	Tom Miles, Capital	5,100	
	Roy Binns, Capital	10,200	
	Fay Salt, Capital	10,200	
	Loss on Disposal of Assets.		25,500
	To record allocation of loss due to		
	disposal of assets in the agreed ratio		
	of 1:2:2.		

May 1	Accounts Payable	16,000	
	Cash		16,000
	To record payment to creditors.		
May 1	Tom Miles, Capital	200	
	Roy Binns, Capital	400	
	Fay Salt, Capital		600
	To record reallocation of loss from		
	Salt's account to remaining partners		
	in accordance with the profit-sharing		
	ratio.		
May 1	Tom Miles, Capital	14,700	
	Roy Binns, Capital	7,400	
	Cash		22,100
	To record distribution of remaining		
	cash to partners.		

The schedule supporting the sale of the assets, payments to creditors, and the final distribution of cash to partners, would appear as follows:

Statement of Liquidation

	Cash +	Other Assets =	Liabilities +	Miles Capital +	Binns Capital +	Salt Capital
	$3,600	$60,000	$16,000	$20,000	$18,000	$9,600
Sale of Accounts						
Receivable	18,000	(22,000)		(800)	(1,600)	(1,600)
Sale of Inventory						
	16,500	(28,000)		(2,300)	(4,600)	(4,600)
Disposal of						
Equipment		(10,000)		(2,000)	(4,000)	(4,000)
Balances after						
Realization	$38,100	-0-	$16,000	$14,900	$7,800	($600)
Payment of						
Liabilities	(16,000)		(16,000)			
Balances	$22,100	-0-	-0-	$14,900	$7,800	($600)
Distribution of Potential						
Additional Loss				(200)	(400)	600
Balances	$22,100			$14,700	$7,400	-0-
Distribution						
of Cash	($22,100)			($14,700)	($7,400)	
	$0			$0	$0	$0

Theme 14 FORMATION AND OPERATION OF THE CORPORATION

A corporation is a separate legal entity authorized by the state of incorporation to conduct business. The corporate charter indicates the number of preferred and common shares that a corporation is authorized to issue. A corporation pays cash and stock dividends to its shareholders. Corporate stockholders' equity consists of outstanding stock (contributed capital) and retained earnings.

INDIVIDUAL KEYS IN THIS THEME

Key 79   Forming the corporation

OVERVIEW *A corporation is a separate legal entity authorized by the state of incorporation to conduct business. Before a corporation can begin doing business it must obtain a charter (also called articles of incorporation) from the state.*

Corporate balance sheet: A corporation's balance sheet consists of assets, liabilities, and a stockholders' equity section.
- The stockholders' equity section (representing ownership) of any corporation balance sheet is considerably different and more complex than that of a sole proprietorship or partnership.
- The shareholders' equity section of the corporate balance sheet is usually divided into two parts: (1) Paid-In Capital (or Contributed Capital) and (2) Retained Earnings.

Key 80   Issuance of stock

OVERVIEW *The corporate charter indicates the number of preferred and common shares that a corporation is authorized to issue. Shares issued to the investing public are called issued or outstanding stock.*

Ownership: Every class of corporate stock represents some basic ownership interest in a corporation.
- When a corporation issues only one class of stock, it is usually common stock. Common stock generally carries the right to vote.
- In order to appeal to all groups of the investing population, corporations may offer both common and preferred stock. Preferred shares give the owners preference over the common shareholders in the event of a dividend payment or a corporate liquidation.

Value: Stock may be issued at par value, at a premium, or at a discount: A corporation can issue stock in return for cash, noncurrent assets such as land, buildings, and equipment, and for organization costs (the costs of organizing the corporation).
- The par value of a share of stock measures the amount that must be paid before the stock can be issued.
- Where the par value of the corporation's stock is not stated in the corporate charter, the shares are classified as no-par value stock.
- In virtually all states, the board of directors is permitted to place a stated value on its no-par value stock. The stated value sets the minimum price at which the no-par value stock may be issued.

KEY EXAMPLE

The Saxon Corporation was organized on May 1. The corporate charter authorizes the issuance of 50,000 shares of $50 par value 8% preferred stock and 100,000 shares of $10 par value common stock. On May 3, Saxon issued 4,000 shares of common stock for $40,000. The journal entry to record the issuance of the stock would be as follows:

May 3	Cash	40,000	
	Common Stock		40,000
	To record issuance of 4,000 common		
	shares at $10 par.		

On May 10, Saxon paid its attorney $100 and gave her 90 shares of common stock in payment for legal fees incurred in organizing the corporation. The journal entry to record the issuance of the stock would be as follows:

May 10	Organization Costs	1,000	
	Cash		100
	Common Stock		900
	To record cash payment and issuance		
	of 90 common shares at $10 par in		
	payment for legal services rendered.		

On May 14, Saxon issued 2,000 shares of its $50 par value 8% preferred stock in return for the following assets: inventory $10,000; land $25,000; building $60,000; and machinery $15,000. The journal entry to record the issuance of the preferred stock in exchange for the noncash assets would be as follows:

May 14	Inventory	10,000	
	Land	25,000	
	Building	60,000	
	Machinery	15,000	
	Preferred Stock		100,000
	Premium on Preferred stock		10,000
	To record issuance of 2,000 preferred		
	shares at $50 par at a premium in		
	return for noncash assets.		

On May 25, Saxon sold 100,000 shares of $10 par value common stock for $90,000. The journal entry to record the issuance of the stock would be as follows:

May 3	Cash	90,000	
	Discount on Common Stock	10,000	
	Common Stock		100,000
	To record issuance of 10,000 common		
	shares with a $10 par value at a		
	discount.		

OVERVIEW *Both common and preferred shareholders usually receive annual dividends, with the preferred share-holders' payments receiving priority.*

Participating stock: Preferred stock that provides for the possibility of an additional dividend in excess of a certain amount is called participating stock.

Cumulative stock: If the preferred stock also carries a right whereby the common shareholders will not receive a dividend until all prior preferred dividends (called arrears or arrearages) have been paid, the preferred stock is said to be cumulative.
- Preferred shares not having this right are called nonparticipating.

Dividends: Dividends are declared and paid by the corporation's board of directors.
- Dividends are paid on a percentage of a stock's par value. This means that preferred 8% stock with a $100 par value pays an $8 annual dividend.

KEY EXAMPLE

The Megow Corporation has outstanding 10,000 shares of $100 par value 10% (meaning a dividend of $10 per share) participating preferred stock and 40,000 $50 par value common shares paying an annual dividend of $5 per share. At year end, the board of directors declared an annual dividend of $500,000. The corporate charter specifies that after payment of the regular dividend to both the preferred and common shareholders, the balance of the dividend payment will be shared ratably on a share-for-share basis based on the total number of all shares outstanding. The distribution of the dividend between the two classes of stock would be as follows:

	Preferred Dividend	Common Dividend	Total Dividends
Regular Dividend Payment to Preferred Shares 10,000 Shares × $10	$100,000		$100,000
Regular Dividend Payment to Common Shares 40,000 Shares × $5		200,000	200,000
Distribution of Balance of Dividend Payment Preferred Shares 10,000 Shares × $4*	40,000		40,000
Common shares 40,000 Shares × $4		160,000	160,000
Total	$140,000	$360,000	$500,000
Dividends Per Share	$14	$9	

*$500,000 dividend less $300,000 regular dividends paid = $200,000 remaining ÷ 50,000 shares (10,000 preferred + 40,000 common) = $4.

Key 82   Treasury stock

OVERVIEW *Treasury shares are preferred or common outstanding shares reacquired by the issuing corporation. Treasury stock, once reacquired, is no longer outstanding.*

Treasury stock: In recording the acquisition of treasury shares, an account called Treasury Stock is debited, and Cash is credited for the purchase price.
- If the treasury stock is subsequently resold, any difference between the selling price and the cost is reflected in an account called Paid-In Capital-Treasury Stock.

KEY EXAMPLE

On November 1, 2002, the Lemon Corporation purchased 1,000 shares of its $10 par value common stock for $15 per share. On November 5, it re-sold 500 of these treasury shares for $20, and on November 30, another 100 shares for $10 per share. The appropriate journal entries to record the purchase and subsequent resale of the treasury shares would be as follows:

Nov. 1	Treasury Stock	15,000	
	Cash		15,000
	To record purchase of 1,000 shares		
	of $10 par value common stock for $15.		
Nov. 5	Cash	10,000	
	Treasury Stock		7,500
	Paid-In Capital-Treasury Stock		2,500
	To record sale of 500 shares of		
	treasury stock at $20 per share.		
Nov. 30	Cash	1,000	
	Paid-In Capital-Treasury Stock	500	
	Treasury Stock		1,500
	To record sale of 100 shares of		
	treasury stock at $10 per share.		

If Lemon had authorized 1,000,000 shares of common stock of which 400,000 were outstanding (of which 400 shares were treasury shares), and Retained Earnings of $50,000, the Stockholders' Equity Section at November 30, 2002, would appear as follows:

Common stock, $10 par; authorized 1,000,000 shares;	
Issued and Outstanding 400,000	$4,000,000
Paid-In Capital-Treasury Stock	2,000
Retained Earnings	50,000
Total Stockholders' Equity	$4,052,000
Less: Treasury Stock (400 shares at cost of $15)	6,000
Total Stockholders' Equity	$4,046,000

Note that certain states, such as California, do not permit treasury stock. In those states not permitting treasury stock, repurchased stock is retired.

Key 83 Retained earnings

OVERVIEW *Retained earnings represent the accumulated but undistributed profits of a corporation earned from its initial date of incorporation. Retained earnings may be further divided into appropriated (or restricted) and unappropriated (or unrestricted) amounts.*

Retained earnings: Accumulated undistributed earnings, or retained earnings, arise from the operations of the corporation. This accumulation is the result of total net income over the years less net losses and dividend payments.

- Where a retained earnings account has a debit balance, balance is known as a *deficit.*
- At the end of the year, the Income Summary account is closed into retained earnings.
- Retained earnings is the last account listed in the stockholders' equity section of the corporate balance sheet.

KEY EXAMPLE

At December 31, the Income Summary account of the Severn Corporation showed a $100,000 credit balance representing profits for the year. The journal entry at December 31 to close the Income Summary account into retained earnings would be as follows:

Dec. 31	Income Summary	100,000	
	Retained Earnings		100,000
	To close Income Summary account.		

If Severn Corporation has a $50,000 operating loss for the year, the journal entry at December 31 would be as follows:

Dec. 31	Retained Earnings	50,000	
	Income Summary		50,000
	To close Income Summary account.		

Key 84   Cash dividends

OVERVIEW *State laws usually require that a corporation have a sufficient credit balance in retained earnings in order legally to enable the board of directors to declare a dividend. The availability of sufficient cash funds is also an important consideration since an unrestricted balance in retained earnings does not ordinarily represent a similar cash balance.*

Cash dividends: A cash dividend paid to shareholders is not tax deductible by the corporation since it represents a distribution of corporate profits and not an expense of doing business.
- A cash dividend, which reduces unrestricted retained earnings, becomes a corporate current liability on the date (called a declaration date) it is declared by the board of directors.
- The dividend is payable to those stockholders who are the owners of the stock on the date of record.
- The payment date represents the date that the stockholders will receive the cash dividend.

KEY EXAMPLE

On September 1, the board of directors of the Platt Corporation had $100,000 in retained earnings, and 10,000 shares of $10 par value common stock. The corporation declared a $10,000 cash dividend to the holders of record on September 10, payment to be made on September 30. The journal entries for the declaration date, date of record, and payment would appear as follows:

Declaration Date:

Sept. 1	Retained Earnings	10,000	
	Cash Dividends Payable		10,000
	To record liability on declaration date.		

Record Date:
Sept. 10 No Entry

Payment Date:

Sept. 30	Cash Dividends Payable	10,000	
	Cash		10,000
	To record payment of cash dividend.		

Key 85   Stock dividends

OVERVIEW *Corporations wishing to "capitalize" retained earnings (meaning to remove from retained earnings into paid-in capital) will issue a stock dividend.*

Stock dividends: A stock dividend does not represent a distribution of corporate assets and, therefore, total stockholders' equity will remain unchanged.
- When recording the declaration of a stock dividend, retained earnings is debited for the fair market value of the stock dividend, and a credit is made to an account called Common Stock Dividends Distributable.
- The account Common Stock Dividends Distributable appears in the Paid-In Capital section of stockholders' equity.

KEY EXAMPLE

On December 1, the Stockholders' Equity section of the Hortense Corporation appeared as follows:

Common Stock, $10 Par Value, 100,000 Shares
    Authorized, 10,000 Shares Issued and Outstanding $100,000
Retained Earnings   200,000
    Total Stockholders' Equity $300,000

On December 10, the corporation declared a 10% stock dividend to the shareholders of record on December 20. On this date, the fair market value of the stock was $14 per share. The shares are to be issued on January 5. The journal entries for the declaration date, date of record, and payment date would appear as follows:

Declaration Date:
Dec. 10 Retained Earnings   14,000
        Common Stock Dividends Distributable   10,000
        Premium on Common Stock   4,000
     To record liability on declaration date
     as follows:
     10,000 shares outstanding × 10% = 1,000 shares.
     1,000 shares × $14 fair market value = $14,000.

Record Date:
Dec. 20 No Entry

On December 31, the stockholders' equity section of the Hortense Corporation would appear as follows:

Paid-In Capital:	
Common stock, $10 Par Value, 100,000 Shares	
Authorized, 10,000 Shares Issued and Outstanding	$100,000
Stock Dividend Distributable	10,000
Premium on Common Stock	4,000
Total Paid-In Capital	$114,000
Retained Earnings	186,000
Total Stockholders' Equity	$300,000

On the payment date in the following year, the journal entry would be as follows:

Jan. 5   Common Stock Dividends Distributable 10,000
         Common Stock   10,000
       To record payment of stock dividend.

After issuance of the common stock, the stockholders' equity section of the Hortense Corporation would appear as follows:

Paid-In Capital:	
Common Stock, $10 Par Value, 100,000 Shares	
Authorized, 11,000 Shares Issued and Outstanding	$110,000
Premium on Common Stock	4,000
Total Paid-In Capital	$114,000
Retained Earnings	186,000
Total Stockholders' Equity	$300,000

Key 86 Appropriations of retained
earnings

OVERVIEW *Appropriations of retained earnings do not reduce cash or retained earnings. Their main purpose is to inform readers that portions of retained earnings are unavailable for the payment of dividends.*

Appropriated retained earnings: Represent restrictions of retained earnings. An appropriation indicates that management does not intend to distribute any dividends equal to the amount of the appropriation because specific assets may be needed for other corporate objectives.

KEY EXAMPLE

On December 31, the board of directors of the Hornsby Corporation, which had retained earnings of $2,000,000 at year-end, voted to appropriate $500,000 for a planned plant expansion program. The journal entry to record the appropriation of retained earnings would appear as follows:

Dec. 31 Retained Earnings   500,000
        Appropriation for Plant Expansion   500,000
        To restrict retained earnings for plant
        expansion.

The retained earnings section of Hornsby's stockholders' equity section would appear as follows:

Retained Earnings:
   Restricted for Plant Expansion $ 500,000
   Unrestricted (or Unappropriated)   1,500,000
Total Retained Earnings $2,000,000

Key 87   Stock splits

OVERVIEW   *When a stock split occurs, it does not change the balance in any ledger account. Both a stock dividend and a stock split increase the number of shares owned by a shareholder.*

Stock split: A stock split does not cause a change in total capital. In a stock split, there is no change in the total dollar amount of capital stock, retained earnings, or total stockholders' equity.

Example: A 2-for-1 stock split will both double the number of shares outstanding and cut the market price of the stock in half. The split is recorded using a memorandum entry.

KEY EXAMPLE

Oct. 1 Memorandum: The corporation, which already had 1,000,000 shares of $10 par value common stock outstanding, issued an additional 1,000,000 shares of its common stock. This reduces the par value of the stock from $10 per share to $5.

Key 88   Book value per share

OVERVIEW *The equity allocated to one share of stock is called book value.*

Book value: Book value of a share of stock is merely a figure appearing on the balance sheet and does not represent the par value or fair market value of the stock.
- If only common stock is outstanding, the book value of a share of stock is simply the total stockholders' equity divided by the number of common shares outstanding.

KEY EXAMPLE

At the year-end, Kermit Corporation has total assets of $3,000,000, total liabilities of $2,000,000, and 5,000,000 authorized shares of $10 par value common stock, of which 1,000,000 shares are outstanding. The book value of each common share is $1, computed as follows:

Total Assets	$3,000,000
Less: Total Liabilities	2,000,000
Stockholders' Equity	$1,000,000

$$\text{Divided by Outstanding Common Shares} \quad \frac{\$1,000,000}{1,000,000} = \$1$$

Note that although the par value of each share is $10, the book value of each share is only $1.

Preferred stock: If the corporation has both preferred and common shares outstanding, the preferred shares must be assigned a value equal to their redemption or par value plus any cumulative dividends in arrears, if applicable.

KEY EXAMPLE

Assume that Marlo Corporation showed the following stockholders' equity section at December 31:

Preferred Stock, $100 Par Value,		
10% Noncumulative and Nonparticipating,		
10,000 Shares Authorized,		
5,000 Shares Issued and Outstanding		$500,000
Common Stock, $10 Par Value,		
25,000 Authorized,		
10,000 Shares Issued and Outstanding	$100,000	
Paid-In Capital on Common Stock	60,000	
Total Capital Attributable to		
Common Stock		160,000
Total Contributed Capital		$660,000
Retained Earnings		95,000
Total Stockholders' Equity		$755,000

The preferred stock is redeemable at $105 per share. The book values of its preferred and common shares would be computed as follows:

Total Stockholders' Equity	$755,000
Less: Equity applicable to preferred shares:	
5,000 shares × redemption price of $105	525,000
Balance applicable to common shares	$230,000
Book value of common shares:	
$230,000 ÷ 10,000 shares =	$23

Theme 15 ANALYSIS OF FINANCIAL STATEMENTS

*F*inancial statement analysis is an attempt to evaluate the operating performance of an enterprise. Ratio analysis provides an indication of a company's strengths and weaknesses and points out areas that need further investigation. The ability of a company to pay its short-term debts is measured by the current ratio, the quick or acid-test ratio, and working capital. Activity ratios measure how quickly certain assets can be turned into cash. Profitability ratios, such as book value per share, return on stockholders' equity, earnings per share, and the price-earnings ratio, evaluate a company's operating performance.

Key 89 How to analyze a financial statement

OVERVIEW *Accountants, financial analysts, and bank officers use various devices in attempting to evaluate a business entity for financial and decision-making purposes.*

Performance: Financial statement analysis is an attempt to evaluate the operating performance of the enterprise. This analysis includes an examination of the financial reports, a review of the company's accounting policies, and ratio analysis. Ratio analysis provides an indication of a company's strengths and weaknesses and points out areas that need further investigation.

Ratios: Financial ratios attempt to measure a firm's operating performance and financial position for both internal decision making and for comparison with other similar businesses. These ratios include
- Liquidity ratios
- Activity ratios
- Profitability ratios

Key 90   Liquidity ratios

OVERVIEW   *Short-term solvency is the ability of a firm to meet its current liabilities as they mature. The ability of a company to pay its short-term debts is measured by the current ratio, the quick or acid-test ratio, and working capital.*

Purpose of liquidity: The aim of liquidity is to have enough funds on hand so as to pay bills as they come due and to meet unexpected cash demands.

- Liquidity ratios include the current ratio, and the acid-test or quick ratio.
- The current ratio is the ratio of total current assets to total current liabilities.
- Many analysts favor a "quick" or "acid-test" ratio that compares total current liabilities with cash, marketable securities, and accounts receivable.
- The quick or acid-test ratio eliminates both inventory and prepaid expenses because there is a question of how quickly these assets can be sold to raise cash.
- Working capital is equal to the excess of current assets less current liabilities.

KEY EXAMPLE

Comparative financial statements of the Wharton Corporation for the years ended December 31:

Balance Sheet

	2004	2003
Assets		
Current Assets		
Cash	$ 100	$ 160
Marketable Securities	1,000	1,000
Receivables-Net	1,800	1,700
Inventories	2,100	2,000
Prepaid Expenses	400	300
Total Current Assets	$5,400	$5,160

Plant and Equipment		
Land, Buildings, Machinery and		
Equipment Net of Accumulated		
Depreciation	6,000	6,200
Total Assets	$11,400	$11,360

Liabilities		
Current Liabilities		
Accounts Payable	$ 1,500	$ 2,000
Notes Payable	900	560
Total Current Liabilities	$ 2,400	$ 2,560
Bonds Payable	600	600
Total Liabilities	$ 3,000	$ 3,160

Stockholders' Equity		
Common Stock ($10 par value: 700 shares)	$ 7,000	$ 7,000
Additional Paid-In Capital	300	300
Retained Earnings	1,100	900
Total Stockholders' Equity	$ 8,400	$ 8,200
Total Liabilities and Stockholders' Equity	$11,400	$11,360

Income Statement

	2004	2003
Sales	$10,900	$10,350
Cost of Goods Sold	6,800	6,900
Gross Margin	4,100	3,450
Selling and Administrative Expenses	2,100	1,450
Income from Operations	$ 2,000	$ 2,000
Provision for Income Taxes	700	900
Net Earnings	$ 1,300	$ 1,100
Average Number of Common Shares		
Outstanding	100	100
Net Earnings per Share	$13.00	$11.00

The current ratio for 2004 would be 2.25, calculated as follows:

Cash	$100	
Marketable Securities	1,000	
Receivables-Net	1,800	
Inventories	2,100	
Prepaid Expenses	400	
Total Current Assets	$ 5,400	= 2.25
Current Liabilities	2,400	

The quick or acid-test ratio for 2004 would be 1.21, calculated as follows:

$$\frac{\text{Cash} + \text{Marketable Securities} + \text{Net Receivables}}{\text{Current Liabilities}}$$

or

$$\frac{\$100 + \$1,000 + \$1,800}{\text{Current Liabilities}} = \frac{\$2,900}{2,400} = 1.21$$

Working capital for 2004 would be $3,000, calculated as follows:

Cash	$ 100
Marketable Securities	1,000
Receivables-Net	1,800
Inventories	2,100
Prepaid Expenses	400
Current Assets	$5,400
Less: Current Liabilities	2,400
Working Capital	$3,000

Key 91   Activity ratios

OVERVIEW *Activity ratios measure how quickly certain assets can be turned into cash.*

Activity ratios: Include the receivable turnover and inventory turnover ratios.
- The receivable turnover ratio measures the quality of the receivables and how efficient the company is in collecting its outstanding receivables.
- The inventory turnover ratio measures how quickly the inventory is being sold. The longer the inventory remains unsold, the greater the chance that it will become obsolete.

Computation 1: The accounts receivable turnover is computed by dividing net sales by average accounts receivable outstanding during the year.

KEY EXAMPLE

The accounts receivable turnover in this example would be 6.23, calculated as follows:

Accounts Receivable January 1	$1,700
Accounts Receivable December 31	1,800
	$3,500
Average Accounts Receivable	$\dfrac{\$3,500}{2} = \$1,750$
Sales	$\dfrac{\$10,900}{1,750} = 6.23$

Dividing 365 days by the turnover amount provides a measure of the average number of days it takes to collect the accounts receivable. This number is then compared with the industry average to determine whether or not the company is maintaining an efficient collection policy. The higher the turnover, the shorter the collection period.

Since the account receivable turnover is 6.23, it would take 59 days (365 – 6.23) to collect the accounts receivable. This amount must then be compared with the industry average to determine whether or not Wharton's collection procedures are effective.

Computation 2: Inventory turnover is computed by dividing net sales into cost of goods sold.

KEY EXAMPLE

Inventory turnover would be 3.32, calculated as follows:

Inventory January 1	$ 2,000
Inventory December 31	2,100
Average Inventory	$\dfrac{\$ 4,100}{2} = \$2,050$
Cost of Goods Sold	$\dfrac{\$ 6,800}{2,050} = 3.32$

Dividing 365 days by the turnover amount indicates how long it takes to sell the inventory. Since the inventory turnover is 3.32, it would take 110 days (365 ÷ 3.32) to sell all of the inventory. This amount must then be compared with the industry average.

Key 92   Profitability ratios

OVERVIEW *A company's ability to survive depends on its ability to earn a satisfactory profit. The book value per share, return on stockholders' equity, earnings per share, and the price-earnings ratio are important tools used to evaluate operating performance.*

Rate of return: The rate of return on stockholders' equity is defined as net income divided by average stockholders' equity.

KEY EXAMPLE

The rate of return would be 15.7%, calculated as follows:

Stockholders' Equity January 1	$ 8,200	
Stockholders' Equity December 31	8,400	
Average Stockholders' Equity	$\dfrac{\$16,600}{2}$	= $8,300

Net Income of $1,300 ÷ $8,300 = 15.7%. This percentage measures the earnings achieved based on the capital provided by the stockholders in the business. Many investors compare this percentage with amounts earned by other similar companies to evaluate the enterprise's performance. A low rate of return might indicate inefficient management.

Earnings per share (or EPS): Measures the ability of a company to pay dividends by measuring the profit earned per share of common stock. For 2004, the company earned $13 per share of common stock as compared to $11 in the previous year.

Price-earnings ratio (or P/E ratio): Measures the relationship of the current market price of the stock to the earnings per share. Assuming that the common shares are selling at a current market price of $90 per share, the price-earnings ratio would be 6 ($90 ÷ $15 EPS). The price earnings ratio is influenced by the earnings and growth of the firm, its dividend payment policy, and a number of other factors. This ratio is useful in comparing a company's earnings with those of other, similar companies.

Theme 16 STATEMENT OF CASH FLOWS

A company must manage its cash so bills can be paid on time and extra dollars either can be put into new equipment or the purchase of inventory, or can be invested to generate additional earnings. A statement of cash flow reports the cash receipts, payments, and net change in cash resulting from the operating, investing, and financing activities of an enterprise during an operating period.

INDIVIDUAL KEYS IN THIS THEME

93 Cash flows

94 Operating activities

95 Investing activities

96 Financing activities

97 Presentation of the cash flow statement

Key 93   Cash flows

OVERVIEW   *A statement of cash flows reports the cash receipts, cash payments, and net change in cash resulting from the operating, investing, and financing activities of an enterprise during an operating period.*

Need for cash. Cash keeps every business alive.
- A company must manage their cash so bills can be paid on time and extra dollars can be put into new equipment, the purchase of inventory, or invested to generate additional earnings.
- A statement of cash flows reports the cash receipts, payments, and net change in cash resulting from the operating, investing, and financing activities of an enterprise during an operating period. The presentation also reconciles beginning and ending cash balances.

KEY EXAMPLE

Acme Corporation earned $100,000 in credit sales, of which $10,000 remained uncollected as of the end of the calendar year. In order to properly reflect the correct cash inflows, $10,000 would have to be deducted from the sales since it represents future cash to be collected.

Key 94   Operating activities

OVERVIEW *Operating activities include the cash effects of transactions that enter into the determination of net income.*

Classifications: These transactions cannot be classified as either investing or financing activities.
- Operating activities include cash received from the sale of goods or services, such as the collection or sale of accounts and notes receivable from customers, interest received on loans, and dividend income.
- Cash paid to acquire inventory, payments of notes payable to suppliers, payments to employees as compensation, and interest paid to creditors are classified as cash outflows for operating expenses.

KEY EXAMPLE

Flash Corporation had cash receipts from the sale of goods of $1,000,000, collections from accounts receivable of $400,000, and interest and dividend income from debt and equity securities of $100,000. Cash payments to acquire materials for the manufacture of goods were $450,000, payments on accounts and notes payable were $150,000, and $100,000 was paid in taxes, duties, and fines. Flash's net cash provided by operations for the year would be $800,000 determined as follows:

Cash received:		
Sale of Goods		$1,000,000
Collection of Accounts Receivable		400,000
Interest and Dividends		100,000
Total cash inflows		$1,500,000
Cash paid:		
Acquisition of Materials	$450,000	
For Accounts and Notes Payable	150,000	
For Taxes, Duties, and Fines	100,000	
Total cash outflows		700,000
Net Cash Provided by Operating Activities		$ 800,000

Key 95 Investing activities

OVERVIEW *Investing activities involve the sale and purchase of long-term assets, marketable securities, and the making of loans to other enterprises.*

Investing activities: Include cash inflow from the sale of property, plant, and equipment used in the production of goods and services, debt instruments or the equity of other companies, and the collection of loans made to other enterprises.
- Cash outflow under this category must result from the purchase of plant and equipment and other productive assets, debt or equity instruments of other entities, and the making of loans to other enterprises.

KEY EXAMPLE

Glasso Corporation sold its plant and equipment for $300,000, and sold all of its stock investment in Rax Corporation, an unrelated entity, for $200,000. It then bought a new plant for $400,000 and made a loan of $40,000 to another company. Glasso's cash, provided by its investing activities, was $60,000 computed as follows:

Cash received:		
Sale of plant and equipment		$300,000
Sale of stock investment		200,000
Total cash inflows		$500,000
Cash paid:		
Purchase of new plant:	$400,000	
Loan to another entity	40,000	
Total cash outflows		440,000
Net Cash Provided		
by Investing Activities		$ 60,000

Key 96   Financing activities

OVERVIEW *Financing activities include the purchase and sale of the company's own stocks and bonds and the payment of cash dividends.*

Financing activities: Involve the sale of a company's own preferred and common stock, bonds, mortgages, notes, and other short- or long-term borrowing.
- Cash outflow classified as financing activities includes the repayment of short- and long-term debt, the purchase of treasury stock, and the payment of cash dividends.

KEY EXAMPLE

Turbo Corporation sold 1,000 shares of its own common stock for $100,000 cash. It also issued another $5,000,000 in preferred stock in return for land and buildings. Turbo then reacquired 10,000 shares of its own common stock for $600,000 and paid a cash dividend of $200,000. Turbo's net cash used in its financing activities was $700,000 computed as follows:

Cash Received:
Sale of common stock	$100,000

Cash Paid:
Reacquisition of common stock	$600,000	
Cash dividend paid	200,000	
Total cash outflow		800,000
Net Cash Used in Financing Activities		$700,000

The issuance of the preferred stock in exchange for the land and buildings is a noncash transaction, which would be noted elsewhere in the financial statements.

Key 97   Presentation of the cash flow
statement

OVERVIEW *Financial Accounting Standards require businesses to include a statement of cash flow in all financial statements that contain both a balance sheet and an income statement.*

Cash flow statements: The primary purpose of the cash flow statement is to present information about a company's cash receipts and cash payments during the reporting period.

KEY EXAMPLE

Comparative Balance Sheets

ASSETS	2004	2003	Increase/Decrease
Cash	$ 92,000	$ -0-	$92,000 Increase
Accounts Receivable (net)	82,000	-0-	82,000 Increase
Land	100,000	-0-	100,000 Increase
Total	$274,000	$ -0-	

Liabilities and Stockholders' Equity

	2004	2003	Increase/Decrease
Accounts Payable	$ 24,000	$ -0-	$24,000 Increase
Common Stock	100,000	-0-	100,000 Increase
Retained Earnings	150,000	-0-	150,000 Increase
Total	$274,000	$ -0-	

Income Statement
for the Year Ended December 31, 2004

Revenues	$444,000
Less: Operating Expenses	240,000
Income Before Income Tax	$204,000
Less: Income Tax Expense	26,000
Net Income	$178,000

Statement of Cash Flows
for the Year Ended December 31, 2004

Cash flow from operating activities:		
Cash flow from sales	$362,000	
Cash payments for operating expenses	(216,000)	
Cash payments for taxes	(26,000)	
Net cash provided by operating activities		$120,000
Cash outflow from investing activities:		
Cash paid to purchase land		(100,000)
Cash flow from financing activities:		
Cash received from the issuance of		
common stock	$100,000	
Cash paid for dividends	(28,000)	
Net cash provided by financing activities		72,000
Net increase in cash and cash equivalents		$ 92,000
Cash at the beginning of the year		-0-
Cash at the end of the year		$ 92,000

Note that the sales of $444,000 was reduced by the accounts receivable balance of $82,000 to arrive at $362,000 in actual cash receipts. The operating expenses of $240,000 were reduced by $24,000 in accounts payable to arrive at $216,000. Net income of $178,000 less the $28,000 cash dividend equals the retained earnings of $150,000. The accounts payable will not be paid until a future period. All other amounts, such as the purchase of land for $100,000 and the sale of common stock for $100,000, were obtained directly from the balance sheet.

A separate schedule reconciling net income to net cash would be presented.

Cash flows from operating activities:		
Net income		$178,000
Add: Adjustments to reconcile net income to net cash:		
Increase in accounts receivable	(82,000)	
Increase in accounts payable	24,000	58,000
Net cash provided by operating activities		$120,000

Theme 17 INTERNATIONAL ACCOUNTING

*T*he typical corporation is becoming more global in focus, and many U.S. firms buy and sell goods and services in the international marketplace. The cost of buying and selling goods and services in another country might be recorded in U.S. dollars, British pounds, Japanese yen, or deutsche marks. The values of foreign currencies in relation to the U.S. dollar rise and fall on a daily basis.

Key 98   Foreign sales

OVERVIEW *When a company makes a sale in a foreign country, it may record the transaction in either United States dollars or the currency of the foreign country.*

Recording a foreign sale in United States dollars: If a sale to a foreign company is recorded on the books of the United States company in dollars, the entry for the sale is also recorded in dollars.

KEY EXAMPLE

On January 1, 2003, the Murphy Company makes a sale on account of inventory for $140,000 to the Royal Company, in London, England. The entry would be recorded as follows:

Jan. 1   Accounts Receivable, Royal Company,
        London, England   140,000
        Sales   140,000
        To record foreign sale in U.S. dollars.

Assuming that payment is received on February 1, the entry to record the receipt of cash would be as follows:

Feb. 1   Cash   140,000
          Accounts Receivable, Royal Company,
            London, England   140,000
          To record payment of receivable in U.S. dollars.

Recording a foreign sale in U.S. dollars with payment made in a foreign currency: If the sale of inventory is to be measured in British pounds, the United States company will be subject to an **exchange gain or loss** because of the fluctuation in foreign currencies in relation to the dollar. A good rule to follow is that if a foreign currency increases in value after a sale is made on account, and payment is to be received in the foreign currency at a later date, the company will enjoy an exchange gain, because the foreign currency has increased in value.

KEY EXAMPLE

On January 1, 2003, the Murphy Company makes a sale on account of inventory for £100,000 to Royal Company, in London, England. Assume that a British pound costs $1.50 (£1 = $1.50) at the date of the sale. The entry would be recorded using British pounds as follows:

Jan. 1   Accounts Receivable, Royal Company,
        London, England   150,000
        Sales   150,000
        To record foreign sale in British pounds at an exchange rate of £100,000 × $1.50 = $150,000.

Assuming that payment is received on February 1, the entry to record the receipt of cash would be as follows:

Feb. 1   Cash   150,000
        Accounts Receivable, Royal Company,
        London, England   150,000
        To record payment of the receivable in British pounds.

KEY EXAMPLE

Using the above data, assume that payment is received on February 1, when the British pound has increased in value to $1.60. The entry to record the receipt of the British pounds, which are now worth more, would be as follows:

Feb. 1   Cash (£100,000 × $1.60)   160,000
        Accounts Receivable, Royal
            Company, London, England   150,000
        Exchange Gain   10,000
        To record receipt in British pounds (of increased value).

The ledger account reflecting the exchange gain would appear as follows:

Exchange Gain or Loss	
	Feb. 1 10,000

If the currency has decreased in value, the company will receive payment in the foreign currency that is worth less, and will therefore incur an exchange loss.

KEY EXAMPLE

Using the above data, assume that payment is received on February 1, when the British pound has decreased in value to $1.40. The entry to record the receipt of the British pounds, which are now worth less, would be as follows:

Feb. 1	Cash (£100,000 × $1.40)	140,000	
	Exchange Loss	10,000	
	Accounts Receivable, Royal		
	Company, London, England		150,000
	To record receipt in British pounds (of lesser value).		

Any exchange gain or loss is reported on the income statement for the year.

Key 99   Foreign purchases

OVERVIEW *When a company makes a purchase in a foreign country, it may record the transaction in either United States dollars or the currency of the foreign country.*

Recording a foreign purchase in United States dollars: If a sale to a foreign company is recorded on the books of the United States company in dollars, the entry for the purchase is also recorded in dollars.

KEY EXAMPLE

On January 2, 2003, the Oggie Company makes a purchase of inventory on account of inventory for $100,000 from the Kobe Manufacturing Company, in Tokyo, Japan. The entry would be recorded as follows:

Jan. 1	Purchases	100,000	
	Accounts Payable, Kobe Mfg.		
	Company, Tokyo, Japan		100,000
	To record foreign purchase in U.S. dollars.		

Assuming that payment is made on February 1, the entry to record the receipt of cash would be as follows:

Feb. 1	Accounts Payable, Kobe Mfg. Company,		
	Tokyo, Japan	100,000	
	Cash		100,000
	To record payment in U.S. dollars.		

Recording a foreign purchase in U.S. dollars with payment made using a foreign currency: If, however, the purchase of inventory is measured in Japanese yen, the United States company will be subject to an *exchange gain or loss* because of the fluctuation in foreign currencies in relation to the dollar. A good rule to follow is that if a foreign currency increases in value after a purchase is made on account, and payment is to be made in the foreign currency at a later date, the company will incur an exchange loss, because the foreign currency has increased in value, making it more costly.

On January 1, 2003, the Oggie Company makes a purchase of inventory on account of inventory for ¥1,000,000 from the Kobe Manufacturing Company, in Tokyo, Japan. Assume that one yen costs $.0080 ($1 = ¥125) at the date of the sale. The entry would be recorded as follows:

Jan. 1	Purchases	8,000	
	Accounts Payable, Kobe Mfg.		
	Company, Tokyo, Japan		8,000

To record foreign purchase in Japanese yen at an exchange rate of ¥1,000,000 × .008 = $8,000.

Assuming that payment is made on February 1, the entry to record the payment of cash would be as follows:

Feb. 1	Accounts Payable, Kobe Mfg. Company,		
	Tokyo, Japan	8,000	
	Cash		8,000

To record payment in Japanese yen.

Using the above data, assume that payment is made on February 1, when the Japanese yen has increased in value to $.0085. The entry to record the payment of the Japanese yen, which are now worth more, would be as follows:

Feb. 1	Accounts Payable, Kobe Mfg.		
	Company, Tokyo, Japan	8,000	
	Exchange Gain or Loss	500	
	Cash		8,500

To record payment in Japanese yen (of increased value).

If the currency has decreased in value, Oggie will make payment in the foreign currency that is worth less, and will therefore incur an exchange gain.

KEY EXAMPLE

Using the above data, assume that payment is made on February 1, when the Japanese yen has decreased in value to $.0075. The entry to record the payment of the Japanese yen, which are now worth less, would be as follows:

Feb. 1	Accounts Payable, Kobe Mfg.		
	Company, Tokyo, Japan	8,000	
	Exchange Gain or Loss		500
	Cash		7,500
	To record payment in Japanese yen (of lesser value).		

Any exchange gain or loss is repeorted on the income statement for the year.

Key 100 Recording exchange gain or loss between accounting periods

OVERVIEW *If financial statements are prepared between the time the foreign transaction is entered into and the time it is paid, and exchange rates have changed, an exchange gain or loss must be recorded at the end of the accounting period such as year-end.*

Recording an exchange gain or loss at the end of the accounting period: The FASB requires that exchange gains and losses be included in determining the net income for the period in which the exchange rate changed. Thus, if the transaction is entered into in one year, but has not been completed as of the balance sheet date, an entry to record any foreign exchange gain or loss must be made at year-end.

KEY EXAMPLE

Assume that on November 1, 2003, Dial Corporation buys auto parts for $45,000 (100,000 DEM) from Hopple Ltd., a German company in Berlin, Germany. Payment is to be made on February 1, 2003. Dial uses a December 31 year-end. Assume further that the transaction is recorded in U.S. dollars but that payments will be made in German marks (DEM). The exchange rates for the period illustrated is as follows:

	Date	Exchange Rate
Date of Purchase	November 1, 2003	US $.45 = 1 DEM
Year-End	December 31, 2003	US $.44 = 1 DEM
Date of Payment	February 1, 2004	US $.47 = 1 DEM

Exchange gain or loss would be calculated as follows:

	Nov. 1, 2003	Dec. 31, 2003	Feb. 1, 2004
Purchase by Dial recorded in U.S. dollars ($.45 = 1 DEM)	$45,000	$45,000	$45,000
Payment to be made in dollars equal to exchange rate ($.44 = 1 DEM) at year-end	45,000	44,000	
Final payment ($.47 = 1 DEM)			47,000
Exchange gain (or loss)	$ -0-	$ 1,000	($ 2,000)

The journal entries reflecting the above exchange gain and loss for the period covered by the transaction would be as follows:

2003

Nov. 1	Purchases (or Inventory)	45,000	
	Accounts Payable, Hopple Ltd., Berlin, Germany		45,000
	To record purchase when DEM = $.45.		
Dec. 31	Accounts Payable, Hopple Ltd., Berlin, Germany	1,000	
	Exchange Gain or Loss		1,000
	To record year-end adjustment when DEM decreased to DEM = $.44.		

2004

Feb. 1	Accounts Payable, Hopple Ltd., Berlin, Germany	45,000	
	Exchange Gain or Loss	2,000	
	Cash		47,000
	To record payment in U.S. dollars when DEM increased to DEM = $.47.		

Theme 18 LONG-TERM INVESTMENTS

*C*ompanies such as corporations sometimes purchase the bonds and stocks of other companies, either for the income-producing benefits (interest and dividends) or for long-term growth. Debt securities, whether short term or long term, are grouped into three separate categories: held-to-maturity, trading, and available-for-sale. Trading securities are always classified as short-term investments and were previously discussed in Theme 8. Equity securities such as common and preferred stocks represent ownership in a corporation. Remember that the intent of management determines whether investments are long or short term.

INDIVIDUAL KEYS IN THIS THEME

101 Held-to-maturity

102 Available-for-sale

103 Accounting for long-term investments in stock

104 Consolidated financial statements

Key 101 Held-to-maturity

OVERVIEW *Only debt securities such as bonds can be classified as held-to-maturity securities because, unlike preferred and common stock, bonds have a maturity date. If the bonds are to be held until their maturity date, they are treated as **held-to-maturity securities**. When purchased by a company, they are recorded at their cost plus any applicable commissions. Held-to-maturity bonds are accounted for at their amortized cost, not their fair market value. Held-to-maturity securities are always given a noncurrent asset classification (long-term assets) unless their maturity date is within one year of the balance sheet date.*

KEY EXAMPLE

On December 31, 2002, the Montague Corporation purchased $500,000 of Sandbag Company five-year bonds for $543,300. The bonds mature on December 31, 2007. The bonds pay 7% annually at the end of each year. Because the bonds were purchased for $543,300, the premium of $43,300 ($543,300 − $500,000) must be amortized over the life of the bonds. Management has elected to use the effective interest method of amortization rather than the straight line method. Because the bonds were bought at a premium, the actual yield of the bonds is only 5%. Management was given the following bond amortization table:

Col. 1 Interest Dates	Col. 2 Stated Interest Revenue at 7%	Col. 3 Effective Interest at 5%	Col. 4 (Cols. 2 − 3) Amortization of Premium	Col. 5 (Cols. 5 + 4) Carry Value of Bond
12/31/02				$543,300
12/31/03	$ 35,000[a]	$ 27,165[b]	$ 7,835	535,465
12/31/04	35,000	26,773[c]	8,227	527,238
12/31/05	35,000	26,362[d]	8,638	518,600
12/31/06	35,000	25,930	9,070	509,530
12/31/07	35,000	25,470	9,530	500,000
	$175,000	$131,700	$43,300	

[a]$500,000 × 7% = $35,000; [b]$543,300 × 5% = $27,165;
[c]$535,465 × 5% = $26,773; [d]$527,238 × 5% = $26,362

The following schedule presents the fair values of the bonds at the year-end 2003 and 2004:

Date	Amortized Cost	Fair Value	Difference
12/31/02	$543,300	$543,300	
12/31/03	535,465	530,000	$(5,465)
12/31/04	527,238	537,500	10,265

The journal entry to record the purchase of the bonds at December 31, 2000 if they are classified as held-to-maturity would be as follows:

Dec. 31, 2002	Held-to-Maturity Securities	543,300	
	Cash		543,300
	To record purchase of bonds.		

The journal entry to record the receipt of interest income and amortization of the premium at December 31, 2003, would be as follows:

Dec. 31	Cash	35,000	
	Interest Revenue		7,835
	Held-to-Maturity Securities		27,165
	To record interest revenue and premium amortization.		

The journal entry to record the receipt of interest income and amortization of the premium at December 31, 2004, would be as follows:

Dec. 31	Cash	35,000	
	Interest Revenue		8,227
	Held-to-Maturity Securities		26,773
	To record interest revenue and premium amortization.		

The bond investment would be reported as a noncurrent long-term investment on the balance sheet for the years 2003 and 2004 and would be as follows:

December 31, 2003	$535,465
December 31, 2004	$527,238

Note that the investor does not set up a separate account for any bond premium or discount.

Assume that the bonds are sold on January 1, 2005, for $530,000. The journal entry recording the sale would be as follows:

Jan. 1	Cash	530,000	
	Held-to-Maturity Securities		527,238
	Gain on Sale of Securities		2,762
	To record gain on sale of the bonds		
	calculated as follows:		

Any gains or losses that result from the sale of held-to-maturity are closed out into Income Summary and would appear on the income statement.

Key 102   Available-for-sale

OVERVIEW *Debt securities not classified as held-to-maturity are classified as available-for-sale. Available-for-sale are reported at fair value. The unrealized gains and losses related to changes in the fair value of available-for-sale securities are recorded in an unrealized holding gain or loss account. This account is reported as a separate component of stockholders' equity until realized. A valuation account called "Securities Fair Value   Adjustment (Available-for-Sale)" is used when either debiting for losses or crediting for gains.*

KEY EXAMPLE

Recording the accounting of a single security classified as available-for-sale,

On January 1, 2002, the Zizmor Corporation purchased $50,000 of Genesee Company five-year bonds for $54,056, paying 10% semi-annually (which means 5% every six months). Interest payment dates are July 1 and January 1. The effective interest rate is calculated to be 8% because the bonds were purchased at a premium. Because the bonds were purchased for $54,056, the premium of $4,056 ($54,056 − $50,000) must be amortized over the life of the bonds using the effective interest method. The bonds are to be treated as held-to-maturity securities to be held until they mature. Management was given the following partial bond amortization table:

Col. 1 Interest Dates	Col. 2 Stated Interest Revenue at 5%	Col. 3 Effective Interest at 4%	Col. 4 (Cols. 2 − 3) Amortization of Premium	Col. 5 (Cols. 5 − 4) Carry Value of Bonds
1/01/02				$54,056
7/01/02	$ 2,500[a]	$ 2,162[b]	338	53,718
1/01/03	2,500	2,148[c]	352	53,366
7/01/03	2,500	2,135[d]	365	53,001
1/01/04	2,500	2,120	380	52,621

[a]$50,000 × 5% = $2,500; [b]$54,056 × 4% = $2,162;
[c]$53,718 × 4% = $2,148; [d]$53,366 × 4% = $2,135

The following schedule presents the fair values of the bonds at the year-end 2002 and 2003:

Date	Amortized Cost	Fair Value	Difference
1/01/02	$54,056	$54,056	
12/31/02	53,718	52,000	$(1,718)

The journal entry to record the purchase of the bonds at January 1, 2002, if they are classified as held-to-maturity would be as follows:

Jan. 1	Available-for-Sale	54,056	
	Cash		54,056
	To record purchase of bonds.		

The journal entry to record the receipt of interest income and amortization of the premium at July 1, 2002, would be as follows:

July 1	Cash	2,500	
	Interest Revenue		2,162
	Available-for-Sale Securities		338
	To record interest revenue and premium amortization.		

The journal entry to record the receipt of interest income and amortization of the premium at December 31, 2002, would be as follows:

Dec. 31	Interest Receivable	2,500	
	Interest Revenue		2,148
	Available-for-Sale Securities		352
	To record interest revenue receivable and premium amortization.		

The bond investment would be reported as a noncurrent long-term investment on the balance sheet for the year ended December 31, 2002, because management wishes to hold the bonds until their maturity date. If management intends to sell the bonds within one year of the balance sheet date, they would be classified as a current asset.

Because the bonds have a fair value of $52,000 at the December 31, 2002, the following journal entry must be made to record an unrealized holding loss:

Dec. 31   Unrealized Holding Loss—
                 Stockholders' Equity   1,718
                     Securities Fair Value Adjustment
                     (Available-for-Sale)   1,718
                 To record drop in value of securities as follows:
                 Cost $ 53,718
                 Fair Value   52,000
                 Decrease in Value $ 1,718

KEY EXAMPLE

Recording a loss on the decrease of a **group (or portfolio)** of available-for-sale securities.

On December 31, 2003, Purdy Corp. owned available-for-sale securities with a cost basis of $200,000 and fair value of $190,000. The adjusting journal entry to record the decrease in value (unrealized loss) would be as follows:

Dec . 31   Unrealized Holding Gain or Loss—
                 Stockholders' Equity   10,000
                     Securities Fair Value Adjustment
                     (Available-for-Sale)   10,000
                 To record drop in value of securities as follows:
                 Cost $200,000
                 Fair Value   190,000
                 Decrease in Value $ 10,000

The balance sheet presentation at December 31, 2003, would be as follows:

Investments
Available-for-Sale securities, at fair value $190,000

Stockholders' Equity
Unrealized Holding Loss   Dr.$ 10,000

The ledger account reflecting the unrealized loss, which would appear as part of stockholders' equity, would appear as follows at December 31, 2003:

Unrealized Loss (Stockholders' Equity)

Dec. 31, 2003 10,000	

Assume that on December 31, 2004, the securities have increased in value to $195,000. The adjusting journal entry to record the increase in value (unrealized gain) would be as follows:

```
Dec. 31   Securities Fair Value Adjustment
              (Available-for-Sale)                    5,000
              Unrealized Holding Gain or Loss—
              Stockholders' Equity                              5,000
           To record increase in value of securities as follows:
           Fair value at Dec. 31, 2003     $190,000
           Fair value at Dec. 31, 2004      195,000
              Increase in fair value        $   5,000
```

The ledger account reflecting the unrealized loss, which would appear as part of stockholders' equity, would appear as follows at December 31, 2004:

Unrealized Loss (Stockholders' Equity)

Dec. 31, 2003 10,000	Dec. 31, 2004 5,000
Bal. 5,000	

The balance sheet presentation at December 31, 2004, would be as follows:

Investments
Available-for-sale securities, at fair value $195,000

Stockholders' Equity
Unrealized Holding Loss   Dr.$ 5,000

OVERVIEW *Available-for-sale securities may be composed of either debt or equity securities that are not classified as either trading or held-to-maturity securities. When equity securities are involved (preferred and common stocks) the percentage of control that the investor (purchasing company) has in the stock of another company (called the investee company) determines the treatment for the investment subsequent to its purchase.*

Accounting treatment for long-term investments is based on the percentage of ownership in the investee company. The required percentages and the accounting treatment are as follows:

Percentage of Ownership in Investment	Method
Less than 20%	Fair Value Method
Between 20% and 50%	Equity Method
More than 50%	Consolidated Statements

Treatment when ownership is less than 20%: When the percentage of ownership in an investee is less than 20%, it is presumed that the investor company has little or no influence over the investee. If the fair value of the investment is known at year end, the investment must be recorded at this amount. Any net unrealized gains or losses related to the changes in fair value are recorded in an Unrealized Holding Gain Loss-Equity account that is reported as part of stockholders' equity.

KEY EXAMPLE

On July 1, 2003, Mocci Inc. purchases 2,000 voting common shares of Englander Ltd. for $20,000. Mocci intends to treat the stock purchase as a long-term investment.

The journal entry to record the investment is as follows:

July 1	Long-Term Investments	20,000	
	Cash		20,000
	To record purchase of long-term investment.		

On December 31, 2003, the fair value of the shares is determined to be $19,000. The entry to record the unrealized loss on Mocci Inc.'s books would be as follows:

Dec. 31	Unrealized Loss on Long-Term Investments:		
	Stockholders' Equity	1,000	
	Allowance to Adjust Long-Term		
	Investment to Fair Value		1,000
	To reduce the long-term investment account to		
	fair value as follows:		
	Cost	$20,000	
	Fair Value	19,000	
	Decrease in value at year end	$ 1,000	

The ledger accounts reflecting the allowance account, which is a contra-asset account, and the unrealized loss, which is part of Mocci Inc.'s stockholders' equity section, would appear as follows at December 31, 2003:

Allowance to Reduce Long-Term
Investments to Fair Value (A Contra Account)

	Dec. 31, 2003	1,000

Unrealized Loss (Stockholders' Equity)

Dec. 31, 2003	1,000	

The balance sheet presentation for Mocci Inc. at December 31, 2003, would be as follows:

Noncurrent Investments
Englander Ltd. at Fair Value (cost $20,000) $19,000

Stockholders' Equity
Unrealized Holding Loss   Dr.$ 1,000

Assume that on May 1, 2004, Englander pays a $1 per share cash dividend. The journal entry would be as follows:

May 1	Cash	2,000	
	Dividend Income		2,000
	To record receipt of cash dividend:		
	2,000 shares × $1.		

On November 30, 1,000 of the 2,000 shares were sold for $8,800. The journal entry to record the sale would be as follows:

Nov. 30	Cash	8,800	
	Loss on Sales of Investments	1,200	
	Long-Term Investments		10,000
	To record loss on sale of half of the		
	long-term investment.		

Note that the allowance account is not adjusted for the sale. Any adjustments to this account are made only at year-end.

Assume that at December 31, 2004, year-end, the remaining investment of 1,000 shares have a fair value at $9,500. The journal entry to adjust the Allowance to Adjust Long-Term Investment to Fair Value account would be as follows:

Dec. 31	Allowance to Adjust Long-Term		
	Investment to Fair Value	500	
	Unrealized Loss on Long-Term Investments:		
	Stockholders' Equity		500

      To reduce the long-term investment account to
      fair value as follows:

Cost of remaining shares	$10,000
Fair Value	9,500
Decrease in value at year-end	$ 500

The ledger accounts reflecting the adjusted allowance account, which is a contra-asset account, and the unrealized loss, which is part of Mocci Inc.'s stockholders' equity section, would appear as follows at December 31, 2004:

Allowance to Adjust Long-Term
Investments to Fair Value (A Contra Account)

Dec. 31, 2004	500	Dec. 31, 2003	1,000
		Bal.	500

Unrealized Loss (Stockholders' Equity)

Dec. 31, 2003	1,000	Dec. 31, 2004	500
Bal.	500		

The balance sheet presentation for Mocci Inc. at December 31, 2004, would be as follows:

Noncurrent Investments
Englander Ltd. at Fair Value (cost $10,000) $9,500

Stockholders' Equity
Unrealized Holding Loss   Dr.$ 500

If the fair value of the long-term investments exceeded their original cost, the unrealized gain would have been completely eliminated. However it is not permissible to increase the value of the long-term assets above their original cost.

Any gains or losses that result from the sale of long-term investments are closed out into Income Summary and would appear on the income statement.

Treatment when ownership is 20% to 50%: Ownership of 20% or more of a company voting stock is considered sufficient to influence the operations of the company. In this case, the purchaser (investor company) must use the equity method of accounting. Under the equity method, the carrying value of the investment must be increased by the investor's proportionate share of any earnings. Any losses and the payment of any cash dividends received must be credited to the investment account. Cash dividends must be used to reduce the investment account because they are considered as representing a return of part of the investment.

On April 1, 2003, Arroyo Ltd. purchases 40% of the voting common shares of Gonzalez Mfg. Inc. for $250,000. Arroyo intends to treat the stock purchase as a long-term investment. Note that with this percentage of ownership, Arroyo is expected to influence both management and the operations of Gonzalez. The journal entry to record the investment is as follows:

Apr. 1   Investment in Gonzalez Mfg. Inc.   250,000
     Cash   250,000
    To record purchase of 40% of the
    voting stock of Gonzalez Mfg. Inc.

On July 15, 2003, Gonzalez declares and pays a cash dividend of $100,000. The journal entry to record the cash dividend is as follows:

Jul. 1   Cash   40,000
     Investment in Gonzalez Mfg. Inc.   40,000
    To record 40% the cash dividend
    (40% × $100,000) under the equity
    method.

Note that the cash dividend must be credited to the Investment in Gonzalez Mfg. Inc. account and not to the Dividend Income account.

At December 31, 2003, Gonzalez Mfg. Inc. earned $300,000 in net income.

The journal entry to record the Arroyo's proportional share of income based upon Gonzalez's net income for the year would be as follows:

Dec. 31   Investment in Gonzalez Mfg. Inc.   120,000
     Income from Gonzalez Mfg. Co.   120,000
    To record Arroyo's proportional share
    of income based upon Gonzales's net
    income (40% × $300,000).

The ledger account reflecting the balance in the Gonzalez Investment account at December 31, 2003, would be $330,000, calculated as follows:

Investment in Gonzalez Mfg. Inc.

Apr. 1	250,000	July 1	40,000
Dec. 31	120,000		
	370,000		
Bal.	330,000		

Any revenue recognized under this method (Income from Gonzalez Mfg. Co. of $120,000) would be reported on Arroyo's income statement.

Key 104 Consolidated financial statements

OVERVIEW *When one company, called the parent, purchases more than 50% of the voting stock of another corporation, called the subsidiary, the purchasing corporation is deemed to have a controlling interest.*

Preparation of Financial Statements: When the parent treats the subsidiary as a long-term investment, consolidated financial statements, rather than individual statements for each company, are prepared. When consolidated financial statements are prepared using a worksheet, the Investment in Subsidiary account is offset against the subsidiary's outstanding common stock and retained earnings by means of an elimination entry.

KEY EXAMPLE

On January 15, 2003, Raceway Ltd. purchased 100% of the voting common stock of Tau Inc. for $100,000. At that date, the balance sheet of each company appeared as follows:

	(Parent Co.) Raceway Ltd.	(Subsidiary Co.) Tau Inc.
Cash	$150,000	$ 20,000
Other Assets	400,000	90,000
Total Assets	$550,000	$110,000
Liabilities	$100,000	$ 10,000
Com. Stk. $10 par value	400,000	50,000
Retained Earnings	50,000	50,000
Total Liabilities and Stockholders' Equity	$550,000	$110,000

Note that at this date, the book value of Tau was $100,000 consisting of common stock of $50,000 and retained earnings of $50,000.

The journal entry to record the purchase on January 15, 2003 would be as follows:

Jan. 15 Investment in Tau Inc. (Subsidiary)   100,000
             Cash   100,000
         To record purchase of subsidiary
         company at book value.

A consolidated balance sheet prepared after the purchase would appear as follows:

Parent and Subsidiary Companies
Work Sheet for Consolidated Balance Sheet
as of Acquisition Date

Accounts	(Parent Co.) Raceway Ltd.	(Sub. Co.) Tau Inc.	Dr.	Cr.	Cons. Bal. Sheet
Cash	50,000	20,000			70,000
Investment in Tau	100,000			a100,000	
Other Assets	400,000	90,000			490,000
Total Assets	550,000	110,000			560,000
Liabilities	100,000	10,000			110,000
Com. Stk. $10 par value	400,000	50,000	a50,000		400,000
Retained Earnings	50,000	50,000	a50,000		50,000
Total Liabilities and Stockholders' Equity	550,000	110,000	100,000	100,000	560,000

Sometimes a subsidiary is purchased for a price above its book value because of goodwill. If Tau was purchased for $125,000, or $25,000 above book value ($125,000 – $100,000), a consolidated balance sheet prepared after purchase would appear as follows:

Parent and Subsidiary Companies
Work Sheet for Consolidated Balance Sheet
as of Acquisition Date

Accounts	(Parent Co.) Raceway Ltd.	(Sub. Co.) Tau Inc.	Dr.	Cr.	Cons. Bal. Sheet
Cash	25,000	20,000			45,000
Investment in Tau	125,000			[a]125,000	
Other Assets	400,000	90,000			490,000
Goodwill			[a]25,000		25,000
Total Assets	550,000	110,000			560,000
Liabilities	100,000	10,000			110,000
Com. Stk. $10 par value	400,000	50,000	[a]50,000		400,000
Retained Earnings	50,000	50,000	[a]50,000		50,000
Total Liabilities and Stockholders' Equity	550,000	110,000	125,000	125,000	560,000

Consolidated Income Statements: Consolidated balance sheets prepared for a parent and its subsidiary require that the income statements also be consolidated. When preparing consolidated income statements, intercompany transactions made between the parent and its subsidiary, such as the purchase and sale of inventory, must be eliminated. Such eliminations are necessary to avoid overstatement of both the sales and purchases accounts.

Assume that on December 31, 2003, the income statements for Raceway Ltd. and Tau Inc. were as follows:

	(Parent Co.) Raceway Ltd.	(Subsidiary Co.) Tau Inc.
Sales	$350,000	$100,000
Cost of Goods Sold	200,000	60,000
Other Expenses	50,000	10,000
Total Cost and Expenses	250,000	70,000
Net Income	$100,000	$ 30,000

During the year Tau bought $25,000 in inventory from Raceway. A consolidated work sheet at December 31, 2003, showing the elimination of intercompany sales and purchases of $25,000 would appear as follows:

Parent and Subsidiary Companies
Work Sheet for Consolidated Income Statement
for the Year Ended December 31, 2003

Accounts	(Parent Co.) Raceway Ltd.	(Sub. Co.) Tau Inc.	Dr.	Cr.	Cons. Bal. Sheet
Sales	350,000	100,000	a25,000		425,000
Cost of Goods Sold	200,000	60,000		a25,000	235,000
Gross Profit	150,000	40,000			190,000
Other Expenses	50,000	10,000			60,000
Net Income	100,000	30,000	25,000	25,000	130,000

GLOSSARY

accelerated depreciation A method of depreciation that results in the highest depreciation charge in the first full year and declining charges in all subsequent years of an asset's use.

account A basic storage section used in accounting systems. Every asset, liability, capital, revenue, and expense account has an account. Accounts are found in the general ledger.

account balance Every account containing entries has either a debit or credit balance. When the debits and credits are footed, and the totals are equal, the account has no balance.

accountant's report Sometimes called the auditor's report. This statement shows the financial condition of the business at a certain period of time. Usually prepared on a quarterly or annual basis.

accounting Rules and methods by which financial data is collected, recorded, and summarized into reports called financial statements. Accounting is often referred to as the language of business.

accounting cycle All the steps necessary to collect, record, and classify business transactions so that financial statements can be prepared at the end of the period.

accounting equation Assets = Liabilities + Capital. This equation reflects the total amounts found on the balance sheet.

accounts receivable Claims against customers and others for merchandise sold or for services rendered. Receivables expected to be collected within one year or within the current operating cycle are classified as current receivables.

accounts receivable turnover This number, which measures how quickly the accounts receivable are being collected, is computed by dividing net sales by average accounts receivable outstanding during the year. The higher the turnover, the shorter the collection period.

accrual basis of accounting

Under this method, financial transactions are recorded in the period that they occur rather than when the entity receives or pays cash.

accumulated depreciation

Accumulated depreciation represents the total depreciation applicable to long-lived assets such as a building or equipment. Accumulated depreciation is a contra-asset account and always has a credit balance. Use of this account allows the original cost of the asset to remain unchanged.

adjusted trial balance

The trial balance of an entity after all adjustments have been made.

adjusting journal entries

Entries made at the end of an accounting period to bring the accounts up to date and to assure the proper matching of costs with revenues.

aging the accounts receivable

The process by which a schedule is prepared classifying how long each account receivable is outstanding. This method is sometimes used to calculate an amount that must be added to the Allowance for Doubtful Accounts at year end.

allowance for doubtful accounts

This contra account is sometimes called the Allowance for Uncollectible Debts account. A credit balance in this account serves to reduce the accounts receivable to their net realizable value.

American Institute of Certified Public Accountants (AICPA)

The national professional association of certified public accountants (CPAs). This organization has played a vital role in developing generally accepted accounting principles (GAAP) and generally accepted auditing standards (GAAS).

amortization

The periodic write-off of intangible assets such as goodwill, patents, and copyrights.

annual report   An entity's annual report contains the financial statements and accompanying notes that summarize the entity's financial activities of the past year and any significant plans for the future.

assets   The economic resources of a business. Assets are both current (cash, accounts receivable, etc.) and noncurrent (land and buildings, etc.).

authorized stock   The amount of preferred and common stock that a corporation may legally issue to the investing public. Stock that has been sold to the public is called authorized and outstanding stock.

available-for-sale securities   Debt and equity securities that do not fall into either of the held-to-maturity or trading securities categories.

balance   The difference, or net result, between the total of the debits and the credits after footing an account.

balance sheet   The balance sheet shows the financial position of a business at a particular date. A balance sheet lists assets, liabilities, and capital (stockholders' equity in the case of a corporation).

balance sheet equation   Assets = Liabilities + Capital.

bank reconciliation   The procedure whereby the differences between the book balance found in the cash ledger account of the depositor and the cash balance per the bank statement are explained.

beginning inventory   The inventory on hand at the beginning of an accounting period. It is the ending inventory found on both the balance sheet and income statement of the prior year's financial statements.

bond   A long-term interest-paying obligation, which is issued by a corporation to the investing public. The account Bonds Payable is found on the balance sheet and bondholders are creditors (not owners) of the corporation.

bond indenture

An agreement between the corporation issuing the bonds and the bondholders that defines the rights and obligations of each party. The bond indenture agreement specifies whether the bonds are secured or not, and the rate of interest that the bonds must pay.

bond issue

The total amount of bonds to be issued by the business entity at one time.

bond sinking fund

A sinking fund is created by setting aside a specified amount of cash at regular intervals for the payment of any bonds outstanding at their maturity. A provision for setting up a sinking fund is found in the bond indenture agreement.

bookkeeping

The process of recording transactions in the books of account. This is the record-making phase of accounting.

book value

Total assets less total liabilities of a company. Book value is also equal to owners' equity.

capital expenditure

Any material payment for plant assets that will benefit several accounting periods.

cash

Cash is money on deposit in banks and any items for immediate deposit. These items include checks, money orders, and charge slips. "Cash-equivalents," which is used for cash flow statements, are short-term, highly liquid investments.

cash basis of accounting

Under the cash basis of accounting, revenue is recorded only when cash is actually received and expenses are recorded only when paid out, to determine whether an enterprise is operating at a profit.

Certified Public Accountant (CPA)

Public accountants who have passed a rigorous professional examination administered by the American Institute of Certified Public Accountants (AICPA) are given a CPA certificate.

chart of accounts	A schedule whereby each account in the general ledger is given an identification number. A chart of accounts may list the name of the account as well as its number.
closing entries	Journal entries that are made at the end of the year that transfer amounts from the income and expense accounts (nominal or temporary accounts) into Income Summary. The Income Summary account is then closed into capital. At year-end, the withdrawal accounts are also closed into capital.
common stock	Instruments of ownership issued by a corporation. Common stock normally carries the privilege to vote and the right to receive dividends.
comparability	The comparability principle requires that an enterprise produce accounting statements in such a way that an individual examining the statements can recognize similarities, differences, and trends over several accounting periods.
compound journal entry	A journal entry having two or more debits or two or more credits.
consignment	Goods in the possession of a consignee for resale to third parties. The consignee has only possession and not title to the goods. Ownership (title) to the goods remains with the consignor.
consistency	To achieve reliable comparability, the company must maintain the same consistent accounting principles over the reported period of time.
consolidated financial statements	Financial statements that reflect the combined operations, including the balance sheet and income statement, of the parent and its subsidiary companies.
contra account	An account whose balance is subtracted from another related asset. In the case of accounts

receivable, the contra asset called Allowance for Doubtful Accounts reduces the accounts receivable to their net realizable value.

corporation   An artificial entity created by the granting of articles of incorporation (or charter) to one or more incorporators. A corporation is a distinct and separate legal entity apart from its shareholders.

cost   The actual or historical cost paid for an asset.

cost of goods sold   The amount paid for inventory that was sold during the accounting period.

cost principle   Recording assets at the price paid at the time they were acquired. Annual depreciation, depletion, and amortization is recorded based upon the associated cost of the asset.

coupon bonds   Coupon bonds have interest coupons attached. Every six months, during the life of the bonds, a coupon becomes due and payable.

credit   The right side of any ledger account.

cumulative preferred stock   Stock on which any prior dividends that where not paid accumulate in the form of arrearages and must be paid before any dividend distribution can be paid to the common stockholders.

current assets   Assets that can be converted into cash within one year, or consumed within the normal operating cycle, are called current assets. Examples include cash, short-term marketable securities, accounts receivable, and inventory.

current liabilities   Liabilities payable within one year are classified as current liabilities. Examples include money borrowed from banks, notes payable (maturity of one year or less), amounts owed to suppliers for goods bought on credit, salaries owed to workers, and taxes payable.

current ratio	The current ratio divides current assets by current liabilities. This indicator measures liquidity, or the company's ability to pay short-term debts as they become due.
debenture bonds	Unsecured bonds issued by a corporation. Their value is based on the general credit of the issuing corporation.
debit	The left side of an account.
declining-balance method of depreciation	A method of accelerated depreciation that results in the highest depreciation charge in the first full year and declining charges in all subsequent years of an asset's use.
deferred revenue	Sometimes called unearned revenue. An advance payment for goods or services to be delivered at some future date.
deficit	A debit balance in the Retained Earnings account that is usually the result of continuous operating losses from previous years.
depletion	The allocation of the cost of a natural resource based upon units (tons) removed from a mine or barrels of oil sold.
depreciable cost	The cost of a depreciable asset less its salvage (residual) value.
depreciation expense	The allocation of the cost of a long-term fixed asset over its estimated useful life.
direct charge-off method	The write-off of a bad debt based upon the actual amount of the account receivable determined to be worthless. This method does not use the account Allowance for Doubtful Accounts.
discount	The customer who pays within a stated period of time receives a cash discount or reduction of the cost of the goods. Discount is also the amount by which the maturity value of a bond exceeds its issue price.

dishonored note

When a note is not paid at its maturity (due date).

dividend

A distribution of either cash or stock to stockholders from the accumulated profits of the corporation. Dividends are not an expense of the corporation.

double declining balance method of depreciation

An accelerated method of depreciation that results in the highest depreciation charge in the first full year and declining charges in all subsequent years of an asset's use. Under this method, the rate of straight line depreciation is doubled and applied to the net realizable value of the asset.

double entry system of accounting

An accounting system that records every transaction by making at least one debit entry and one credit entry (equal in total dollar amount) to applicable accounts.

earnings per share (net earnings per common share)

Net income divided by the total number of common shares outstanding. Used by investors as a measure of profitability and comparison with other similar companies.

ending inventory

Unsold merchandise on hand at the end of an accounting period.

equity

Assets less liabilities equals the owner's residual interest.

equity method of accounting

A method of accounting that must be used by an investing company when it holds between 20% and 50% of the voting stock of the investee company. Under this method the investment is increased by the investor's proportionate share of income, whereas a proportionate share of operating losses and cash dividends received reduce the investment account.

estimated useful life

The approximate life expectancy of a long-term asset measured in terms of productive years or units expected to be produced.

exchange rate	The rate at which one currency can be exchanged into the currency of another country.
expenses	Expenses are the cost of the merchandise sold or the services used up in earning revenue. The recording of an expense is always made with a debit entry and causes a reduction in owner's equity.
fair value	The amount that a willing buyer will pay for an instrument.
Financial Accounting Standards Board (FASB)	An independent nongovernmental body charged with the responsibility of developing and issuing accounting standards.
financial position	The balance sheet of a company at a given point. The financial position of a company can also be viewed as the economic resources (assets) less economic claims (liabilities) against the entity.
financial statement analysis	Methods and techniques used in determining the "quality" of the earnings (meaning whether the profits are higher or lower than other companies), and whether the company will continue to be solvent. Various types of analysis, such as the current and acid-test ratios, are used by stockholders and creditors to evaluate the performance of the company.
financial statements	The balance sheet, income statement, and statement of owner's equity.
financing activities	A specific section found on the statement of cash flows. Financing activities consist of a company's transactions with its owners (the sale of common stock) and long-term creditors (sale of a company's bonds).
First-in, First-out (FIFO)	An inventory costing method under which the costs of the first items purchased are assigned to the first items sold. Under this method, the most recent inventory costs are assigned to ending inventory.

fiscal-year

Any twelve-month accounting period used by a business entity.

F.O.B. (free on board) destination

Under this shipping term, the seller pays the cost of shipping the goods to the buyer's place of business.

footing

To add a column of numbers.

freight-in

Additional costs incurred in transporting merchandise (inventory) that will eventually be resold.

full disclosure

An accounting convention requiring that all financial statements contain information and footnotes so as to enable the reader to interpret the statements.

general journal

A basic journal that can be used for any type of journal entry.

general ledger

A book containing all the company accounts of a business.

generally accepted accounting principles (GAAP)

Generally accepted accounting principles are a set of guidelines and procedures that constitute acceptable accounting practice at a given time. They are developed by accountants and businesses to serve the needs of the users of the financial statements.

going concern concept

The assumption that a business will continue to operate. Under this concept, the fair market value of the company's assets is not of primary importance, because the company has no intention of liquidating.

goods available for sale

Beginning inventory plus all inventory purchases.

goodwill

The excess cost over the fair market value of a group of assets. Goodwill is the result of the excellent reputation of the company, the quality of its products, and the amount of time in business. Amortizable over a reasonable period of time not to exceed forty years.

gross margin — Gross margin, or gross margin on sales, is sales less the cost of goods sold. Gross margin less operating expenses results in net income.

gross sales — Total sales, including cash sales and sales on credit, for an accounting period.

held-to-maturity securities — Debt securities that a company has the ability and intent to hold to maturity.

income statement — A financial statement that summarizes operations for a specific period of time, such as one operating quarter (three months) or a year.

income summary — A temporary account used in the closing process. All revenues earned, and all expenses recorded for the period, are closed into the income summary account.

income tax expense — An account that represents all federal, state, and city taxes that appear on the income statement.

intangible assets — Long-term assets that have no physical substance. They include goodwill, copyrights, and patents that are subject to amortization.

interest — The cost of borrowing money. For example, bondholders receive interest.

internet — The world's largest computer network which gives a computer, by means of a modem and an Internet service provider (ISP), access to other computers and web sites.

internal control — A system instituted by management to safeguard the assets of the company and to ensure the accuracy and reliability of the financial records.

inventory turnover — The inventory turnover ratio measures how quickly the inventory is being sold. The longer the inventory remains unsold, the greater the possibility that it will become obsolete.

investing activities A specific section found on the statement of cash flows. Investing involves the making and collecting of loans, the purchasing and selling of plant assets, and the purchases of debt securities (bonds) of other companies.

investments Assets, in the form of stocks and bonds issued by other companies, purchased by management with the intent of earning income and for long-term growth.

issued stock The authorized stock of a corporation that has been sold to investors.

journal A book where entries are made in chronological order.

journalizing The procedure of making entries in a journal.

liabilities The legal obligations of a business that are the result of past transactions or events.

The Limited Liability Company A limited liability company (or LLC) is a hybrid business organization that combines the characteristics of corporations and partnerships.

liquidity The financial ability of having enough cash on hand to pay legal obligations as they become due and to provide for the unanticipated cash demands or opportunities arising out of the business.

long-term liabilities Debts of the business that are payable more than one year after the balance sheet date or beyond the operating cycle of the business.

lower of cost or market A rule for valuing ending inventory. If the market value (replacement cost) is below cost, then market must be used to value ending inventory.

market The current replacement cost used for valuing ending inventory.

marketable securities	Stocks and bonds issued by other companies and purchased by investors for income and long-term appreciation purposes.
market price	The price that investors are willing to pay for stocks and bonds sold on the open market.
matching costs with revenues	The rule whereby revenues must be assigned to the period in which they are earned and expenses must be recorded in the period they are incurred.
materiality	The rule that a transaction is material if its inclusion or omission from the financial statements would influence or change the decision of management.
maturity date	The due date of a promissory note or bond.
maturity value	The total value, consisting of principal and interest, that must be paid at the maturity value of the instrument.
mortgage	A long-term debt, payable in monthly installments, that is secured by the assets of the issuing entity.
net assets	Assets less liabilities. This amount is also equal to owner's equity.
net income (or net loss)	Income minus (cost of goods sold + operating expenses) = net income or net loss.
net loss	The excess of cost of goods sold and operating expenses over income. A net loss results in a decrease in owner's equity.
net realizable value	The proceeds that are realized from the sale of an asset.
nominal accounts	Temporary accounts, such as income and expenses, which are closed into income summary, and withdrawals, which are closed into capital at the end of an accounting period.

noncash investing and financing activities

Major investing and financing activities of an enterprise that do not involve cash inflows or outflows. A schedule of these transactions is found in the statement of cash flows.

noncumulative preferred stock

If a dividend paid on this type of stock is not declared in a given period, it is lost forever to the stockholders.

operating activities

A specific section found in the statement of cash flows. Operating activities involve the purchase of merchandise, the sale of goods and services to customers, and expenses incurred in generating income.

organization costs

The costs, including legal fees and state incorporation fees, of forming a corporation. Organization costs are intangible assets that are expensed as incurred.

outstanding stock

The authorized stock of a corporation that has been issued to its stockholders.

owner's equity

Assets – liabilities = owner's or residual equity.

paid-in capital (contributed capital)

The authorized and outstanding preferred and common stock purchased by the stockholders. Paid-in capital is part of the stockholder's equity on the corporate balance sheet.

par value

An arbitrary amount assigned to both preferred and common stock.

parent company

A company, also known as an investor company, that owns a controlling interest in a subsidiary (investee) company.

participating preferred stock

Preferred stockholders have the right to receive additional dividends after payment of a stated amount to both the preferred and common stockholders.

partnership

An unincorporated business consisting of two or more owners.

partnership agreement	A consensual contract between two or more individuals stipulating, among other things, the name, location, required capital contribution, and distribution of profits and loss among the partners.
patent	An intangible asset giving the owner an exclusive right, for twenty years, to manufacture and sell a specific product.
permanent accounts	The assets, liabilities, and capital of an entity. Permanent, or real, accounts are never closed into income summary.
petty cash	A fund used to pay minor expenditures.
physical inventory	A detailed schedule of the inventory on hand at the end of an accounting period.
post-closing trial balance	A trial balance taken after all income and closing entries have been made.
preferred stock	Stock that gives its owner priority as to dividends, and the right to receive corporate assets before any other stockholders in case of a corporate liquidation.
premium	The amount paid for bonds in excess of the face value of the issue, or the amount paid for a share of stock in excess of its par value.
prepaid expenses	Expenses paid in advance that will not expire in the current year. Prepaid expenses is a current asset.
price-earnings ratio (P/E)	The ratio that compares the current market price of the stock with the earnings per share.
promissory note	An unconditional promise to pay a definite sum of money on demand at a future date.
property, plant, and equipment	Tangible long-term assets used in the operations of a business.

public accounting	That branch of accounting that offers services such as auditing, tax planning, and advisory services to the public for a fee.
Public Company Accounting Oversight Board (PCAOB)	Regulates and oversees audits of public companies by registered accounting firms.
purchases	An account used under the periodic method of recording purchases of merchandise for resale.
purchase discount	The granting of a reduction in the purchase price of merchandise purchased for resale if the purchaser pays early.
quick (or acid-test ratio)	A ratio that compares the total of cash, short-term marketable securities, and net realizable receivables with current liabilities as a measure of liquidity. The quick ratio excludes inventory and prepaid expenses.
ratio analysis	A technique showing the relationships between certain components shown on the financial statements.
real (or permanent) accounts	The assets, liabilities, and capital accounts that are not closed out into income summary at the end of an accounting period.
receivable turnover	The relationship of net sales to average accounts receivable. The turnover measures the efficiency of the collection procedures of a company and shows how quickly the accounts receivable were converted into cash during an accounting period.
registered bonds	Bonds issued by a company in the name of the owner.
retained earnings	A corporation's accumulated earnings and profits. Retained earnings are increased by operating profits and reduced by operating losses and the payment of dividends.

return on common stockholders' equity   The net income of a company is divided by owner's equity to measure the profitability of the company.

revenue   The increase in owner's equity caused by the sale of goods and services.

sales discount   A reduction in the sales price of merchandise offered to a customer as an inducement to make prompt payment.

salvage value   The estimated residual value of a long-term asset.

Securities and Exchange Commission (SEC)   A federal agency that issues accounting releases and administers federal securities laws.

serial bonds   Bonds that mature over several periods of time.

short-term note payable   A note due within one year from the date of the balance sheet.

spreadsheet   A software program consisting of grids made up of rows and columns into which are placed numbers or formulas for use by management in creating documents such as a balance sheet and income statement.

statement of cash flows   A financial statement that reports the cash inflows and outflows for an accounting period and classifies that data into operating, investing, and financing activities.

statement of owner's equity   A statement that shows the changes in owner's equity caused by operating profits and losses, as well as additional investments and withdrawals for a stated period of time.

stock dividend   Additional shares of a corporation's own stock issued to the stockholders.

stock dividend distributable   A stock dividend declared by a corporation's board of directors, but not yet paid. This account is presented in the paid-in capital section of stockholders' equity on the corporate balance sheet.

stock split
An increase in the number of outstanding shares accompanied by a corresponding reduction in the par value of each share of stock.

stockholders' equity
The owner's equity of a corporation that consists of paid-in capital and outstanding preferred and common stock.

straight line depreciation
A depreciation method used for long-term assets that records equal amounts of annual depreciation for each year that the asset is in use.

subsidiary
A corporation, also known as an investee, whose stock is owned by a parent company.

subsidiary ledger
A separate book for all individual accounts receivable and another for all individual accounts payable listed in alphabetical order. The total of each subsidiary ledger must tie in to the accounts receivable and accounts payable account balances in the general ledger.

sum-of-the years digits (SYD)
An accelerated method of depreciation that results in the highest charge in the first full year and declining charges in all subsequent years of the asset's use.

taxable income
The net income of a business upon which the applicable federal, state, or city tax is based.

temporary (or nominal) accounts
The income, expense, and withdrawal accounts that are closed out at year-end.

term bonds
Bonds that mature at the same time.

transaction
Any event that affects the financial position of a company.

trading securities
Debt securities that management intends to sell in the near future in order to generate a profit.

uncollectible accounts expense	The cost that arises from the failure to collect an account receivable.
unearned revenue	A liability that arises when payment is made in advance of goods to be shipped or services to be provided to a customer.
units-of-production method	A depreciation method based upon the number of units produced by a long-term asset.
useful life	The estimated service life of a long-term depreciable asset.
withholding taxes	Social Security, federal, and state taxes deducted from the gross wages paid to an employee.
work sheet	A columnar document used to facilitate the preparation of financial statements at the end of an accounting period.
working capital	The excess of current assets over current liabilities.

INDEX